T0036801

RUNE
READING
YOUR LIFE

RUNE READING YOUR LIFE

A TOOLKIT FOR INSIGHT, INTUITION, AND CLARITY

\ | / /

DELANEA
DAVIS

/ | \ \

FOREWORD BY SARA DAVES

North Atlantic Books
Berkeley, California

Published by
North Atlantic Books
Huichin, unceded Ohlone land
aka Berkeley, California

Cover design by Jasmine Hromjak
Book design by Happenstance Type-O-Rama
Printed in Canada

Rune Reading Your Life: A Toolkit for Insight, Intuition, and Clarity is sponsored and published by North Atlantic Books, an educational nonprofit based in the unceded Ohlone land Huichin (aka Berkeley, CA) that collaborates with partners to develop cross-cultural perspectives; nurture holistic views of art, science, the humanities, and healing; and seed personal and global transformation by publishing work on the relationship of body, spirit, and nature.

North Atlantic Books' publications are distributed to the US trade and internationally by Penguin Random House Publishers Services. For further information, visit our website at www.northatlanticbooks.com.

Library of Congress Cataloguing-in-Publication Data
Names: Davis, Delanea, 1975– author.
Title: Rune reading your life : a toolkit for insight, intuition, and
   clarity / Delanea Davis ; foreword by Sara Daves.
Description: Berkeley, California : North Atlantic Books, 2020. | Includes
   index. | Summary: "In three practical sections, Rune Reading Your Life
   provides an introduction to the 24 runic symbols and their history,
   explains their ancient meanings, and reveals their modern
   interpretations. It guides readers on a 30-day transformational rune
   reading practice, showing how to read, interpret, and apply runic wisdom
   to everyday life."— Provided by publisher.
Identifiers: LCCN 2020003768 (print) | LCCN 2020003769 (ebook) | ISBN
   9781623174514 (hardcover) | ISBN 9781623174521 (ebook)
Subjects: LCSH: Runes—Miscellanea.
Classification: LCC BF1779.R86 D38 2020 (print) | LCC BF1779.R86 (ebook)
   | DDC 133.3/3—dc23
LC record available at https://lccn.loc.gov/2020003768
LC ebook record available at https://lccn.loc.gov/2020003769

2 3 4 5 6 7 8 9 MARQUIS 27 26 25 24 23 22

North Atlantic Books is committed to the protection of our environment. We print on recycled paper whenever possible and partner with printers who strive to use environmentally responsible practices.

CONTENTS

PART I: INTRODUCTION TO THE RUNES

PART II: THIRTY DAYS OF PRACTICE

PART III: MODERN MEANINGS OF THE RUNES

PART IV: MOVING FORWARD

FOREWORD

I am incredibly honored to write the foreword for this book. There is an ethereal richness in runic study that spans millennia. This ancient use of symbols can help bring us into the awareness of the inner workings of the universe—the behind-the-scenes unfolding of our destined life path, which also pays homage to the breadth and fullness of our free will. In this book, you will learn about the history of runes and how these symbols can be used to uncover what cannot be revealed through logical deduction.

The rise of the patriarchy gave us the gift of logic through the written word. But this gift came with a price. Linear thinking became the dominant function and eventually rewired the human mind, revolutionizing the collective consciousness. However, 98 percent of our brain does not use language, logic, and belief. The linear mind makes up 2 percent of our brain, and its function is to organize the data that the other 98 percent—the relational part of our brain—collects through other means. In utilizing only 2 percent of this highly functional supercomputer, we've collectively lost our sensing intelligence, our ability to feel the world around us.

The runes serve as a communication portal of sorts, to assist in articulating what the sensing intelligence knows and helping us go beyond what is possible with mere logic. Incorporating these symbols into a daily practice is a wonderful way to grow the subtle body and focus our attention on daily synchronicities that are unfolding around us in each moment.

My favorite example of sensing intelligence is the ingenuity of the ancient Polynesians, who navigated the ocean without modern-day tools. The Polynesians used their intuition to travel hundreds of miles in canoes by intricately connecting to nature—the waves, currents, clouds, wind, and stars. They could tell that land was nearby without even being able to see it because they were at one with natural forces. They passed this gift down through generations until it became part of their collective consciousness. This ability represents the mastery of the divine feminine essence.

Ancient runic practice is part of this collective conscious awareness of the divine feminine essence. It was meant to be that Delanea would eventually write this book and share her insight into the runes with the world. She has a keen ability to apply the energies of both the divine feminine and the divine masculine, and she can use them to create in the external world. This is the way of the goddess.

I met Delanea in a virtual psychology class in graduate school. She went on to build a business that would uplift the consciousness of corporate environments by teaching mindfulness and spiritually based practices. I am amazed by her courage and ability to successfully communicate her message in masculine-oriented corporate structures and systems.

A few years after our class together, I took a trip to Connecticut to visit her. In those few days, Delanea introduced me to the runes. I was intrigued. I was familiar with receiving messages through tarot readings and other oracles, but I had never used runes before. We talked at length about the runes and other holistic modalities, and our friendship blossomed.

On the last day of my visit, I went to her office for a Reiki session. The channeled messages conveyed during that session changed my life, and I left Connecticut a different person. I am forever grateful to Delanea and the others present that day who set me on the path toward my healing journey.

That experience was the catalyst for my recollection of what I call goddess essence: the communion of the masculine and feminine dynamic. We all have this knowing. It is not something we need to learn; it is instead what we need to remember.

We are constantly playing and working with duality on this plane, and herein lies the ultimate duality: the push and pull between masculine and feminine energies. The union of these dynamics supports the recognition of wholeness. There is great power to be discovered when we learn how to harmonize these energies.

The societal systems ingrained in the collective consciousness do not make it easy for us to find harmony in this way. The power of the feminine has been long forgotten. With the rise of the patriarchy came the colonization of the goddess. This is what all colonization is: the desire to make the feminine like the masculine. Colonization was designed to perpetuate obedience, but the wild divine feminine essence cannot be suppressed. The oppression of the mysterious feminine eventually evoked a collective uprising of women against the masculine. In our quest for equal rights as women, we became socialized to disown our femininity, and we have instead served as a mirror to the shadow aspect of the masculine dynamic.

The message women heard was that not only must we do everything men can do, but we have to do it better. Instead of finding flow in receiving, we decided we must do it all ourselves. The outcome of all that effort is that most women are completely drained and exhausted. We learned that the feminine dynamic is not valuable, yet we still exist in the shadow side of it, because fundamentally it is us. We see the shadow side of the feminine expressed as criticism, trickery, gossip, catastrophizing, depression, and silence.

When the feminine essence goes unacknowledged, so do intuition, collaboration, community, awareness, receptivity, love—all the parts of ourselves we are expected to abandon in the workplace in order to excel in our careers. As women, this puts us at risk of losing touch with our inner power and becoming empty shells.

As societal values shifted toward the masculine, we removed feelings from the equation, increasing surface-level efficiency and effectiveness—the two primary objectives of the Industrial Revolution. We are still under this spell. The less feminine you appear in a corporate environment, the more valuable you are considered to be. We have become experts at using masculine energy to manifest.

The healthy masculine aspect focuses on doing. It takes action in the world. It is logical, goal-oriented, proactive, protective, assertive, competitive, and externally focused. While masculine essence is crucial for creation, in the absence of the feminine, it creates an imbalance in humanity as a whole. Humanity has learned to push, fight, and force desires into manifestation. This is how wars are made.

There is another way: the way of the goddess.

Freya, the goddess mentioned in this book, represents love, beauty, abundance, and destiny. She brought shamanic teachings to the Norse tradition and exuded copious amounts of courage and sensuality. She was so powerful that her very presence was intimidating, even to the gods. In an effort to dilute her power, she was branded as promiscuous. This shame tactic is still used today. One of the surest ways to silence a woman and strip her of her power is to attack her sexuality, either physically or emotionally. This act destroys cultures.

The feminine aspect is wild, free, mysterious, and powerful, representing sensuality, receptivity, awareness, and intuition. As women, we have a direct connection to the moon phases and to Mother Earth. We innately flow with the current of universal laws, and we have a direct influence on the health of the planet. We are also emotional beings, which means we have the power to direct energy using e-motion (energy in motion). Our sensual energy is the most powerful tool we have to create in the world and manifest in the physical.

If we want to awaken the goddess within, we must reclaim our feminine essence.

Goddess energy manifests when the divine masculine and divine feminine meet. Put simply, it is the omnipotent force derived from the merging of the divine masculine and divine feminine energies within. This primal force becomes the foundation of self-mastery, and the harmonic flow of these energies supports manifestation in the material world. We gain the ability to manifest in ways that were once incomprehensible.

This book is timely because we are now waking up to the ancient ways of the goddess, and she is rising. She asks you to stop ignoring your intuition and embrace your innate wisdom. She asks you to use your breath, imagination, and feelings to discover the hidden depths of your connection to everything—to step into the unknown and courageously receive.

In order to receive, we must surrender, which requires faith in ourselves and the universe at large. Surrender is the ultimate spiritual practice. When you release resistance and allow, you will receive the messages you need to hear that will guide you toward alignment with the highest good for all. The runes help you ask the right questions, "why" and "what," while allowing the "how" to unfold. This is the practice of trusting the universe, god, or our source connection.

Runic practice is a way to develop the intuition. It cultivates the art of allowing, receiving, and working with what we can't see—the true embodiment of the divine feminine. Women have the natural ability to work with the darkness, with what cannot be seen. In the darkness there is nothing; yet out of the darkness came everything.

You will read about Delanea's experience in meditation and how she allows images to form in the mind's eye when guidance is needed. With practice, you can also begin to hear what your inner guidance system is revealing to you.

I challenge you to read this book with the wonder and curiosity of a child. Allow your imagination to play with the information. Use the runes to help unlock your internal guidance system. Use them to practice self-love and self-understanding.

All the knowledge you need is already within you. You have the magic of the divine feminine at your fingertips. Happy reading, gods and goddesses.

—SARA DAVES,
intuitive purpose coach,
SaraDaves.com

ACKNOWLEDGMENTS

This book is dedicated to those lives who have been impacted by mental illness. My life was profoundly impacted when two mothers, Melissa and Dianne, lost their battles with addiction. With each loss came profound personal and spiritual growth and my desire to help others work through their pain to discover the innate gifts and blessings we each possess. We all come to this earth with a purpose. May this book inspire you to find yours and share your infinite love with the world.

Ten percent of profits will be donated to the Safe America Foundation, a nonprofit whose mission is to raise awareness and reduce threats of issues including the opioid crisis, human trafficking, and suicide prevention.

INDEX OF RUNES

SYMBOL	PROTO-GERMANIC NAME	ONE-WORD MEANING	CORRESPONDING LETTER	PAGE NO.
ᚠ	*Ansuz*	Signals	A	182
ᛒ	*Berknan*	Growth	B	184
ᚲ	*Kanu*	Opening	C, K, Q	186
ᛗ	*Dægaz*	Breakthrough	D	188
ᛗ	*Ehwaz*	Movement	E	190
ᚠ	*Fehu*	Abundance	F	192
ᚷ	*Gebo*	Partnership	G	194
ᚺ	*Hagalaz*	Disruption	H	196
ᛁ	*Isaz*	Stillness	I	198
ᛃ	*Jera*	Harvest	J	200
ᛚ	*Laguz*	Flow	L	202
ᛗ	*Mannaz*	The Self	M	204
ᛏ	*Naudiz*	Constraint	N	206
ᛟ	*Opila*	Separation	O	208
ᛈ	*Perth*	Initiation	P	210
ᚱ	*Raido*	Journey	R	212

SYMBOL	PROTO-GERMANIC NAME	ONE-WORD MEANING	CORRESPONDING LETTER	PAGE NO.
ϟ	*Sowilo*	Wholeness	S	214
↑	*Teiwaz*	Warrior	T	216
∩	*Uruz*	Strength	U	218
ᚹ	*Wunjo*	Joy	V, W	220
ᚦ	*Thurisaz*	Gateway	TH	222
ᛉ	*Eihwaz*	Surrender	Y	224
Ψ	*Algiz*	Protection	Z	226
ᛜ	*Ingwaz*	Fertility	NG	228
Blank	None	The Unknown	None	230

ABOUT THIS BOOK

Hello and welcome to the wisdom of the ancient runes! Runes are a great tool for helping us learn about ourselves, the people in our lives, and the world around us. Recognized for centuries as both an alphabet and as a communication tool for gaining higher-level perspective, the runes provide us a method to pause and consider what is happening in our lives so we can access our internal compass that desperately wants to guide us.

As a serial entrepreneur who enjoys mentoring others, both precareer and midcareer, I often hear people say, "I don't know what I want," "I don't know what to think," and "I don't know what will make me happier." When we lose track of who we are in the hustle and bustle of life, we may unintentionally morph into what everyone wants us to be rather than staying true to who we really are. Many of us try very hard to meet or exceed the expectations of our parents, our friends, our romantic interest, or even our kids. It can be, in a word, exhausting.

Over time, we may feel isolated or depleted. Somehow, the harder we try, the more lost we can feel. This is a sign that we have become completely disconnected from our authentic selves. Finding our way back to ourselves is easier than you may think. We must simply learn to reconnect to that voice inside us that knows who we are, has all the answers, and remembers what we wanted to be when we were little kids dreaming of being all grown up.

If my words are resonating with you, this book is dedicated to you. As you learn about the runes and discover how to use them to "decode" yourself, you will quickly open up your own intuitive connection between yourself and that all-knowing Inner You. As you develop and strengthen this connection in just thirty days, it will become easy to know yourself—and more importantly, to stay true to yourself. With self-assurance and conviction, you can proceed down your path to a more authentic, meaningful life.

Over the next thirty days, you can work with the runes to do the following:

- **Develop clarity about priority areas in your life.** Explore questions such as: Do you have enough time for family? Rest and relaxation? Play time just for you?

- **Make decisions more quickly and with confidence.** Gradually move away from asking everyone else about what is best for you. Discover that no one knows better than *you* about what is best for *you.*

- **Communicate what you need to others.** Many of us value social harmony, leading us to sometimes avoid saying how what we feel and asking for what we need in an effort to keep the peace. Once we are reminded who we really are deep down, it becomes easier to speak our truth without fear of negative consequences.

Some consider the runes as a conduit between humans and a divine realm where a higher power shares wisdom and protective advice with us. My creative, spiritual side likes this explanation. However, my inner scientist is also drawn to the rational explanation that the runes provide a method for distracting the critical mind, allowing the unrestrained creative mind to see alternatives we may miss when rushing around in our daily lives.

Ultimately, if you experiment with using the runes and it leads to a positive outcome, the reason why it works doesn't really matter. Be your own judge, and base your conclusions on your own personal experience. Runes are just one of many methods you can use for insight and introspection. Of all the methods I've tried, the runes remain my favorite.

I hope you will take the next thirty days to get better acquainted with your inner self and learn what you need to live life authentically, without fear of judgment from yourself or others. We are all here in human form to learn and grow.

Some of us understand and retain information better when we see it, while others prefer to hear it. I encourage you to consider which system of learning is best for you.

Are you an auditory learner? Auditory learners tend to have these characteristics:

- communicate more effectively by speaking
- prefer to hear something rather than read it
- remember how something sounds versus how it looks
- imagine voices and tones
- remember things by talking to themselves

Or are you a visual learner? Visual learners tend to display these traits:

- communicate more effectively by writing
- prefer to read something rather than hear it
- remember what they read or see versus what they hear
- imagine things with pictures and scenes
- remember things by visualizing a scene

If you are a visual learner, then books are your thing. This book provides all you need to learn rune reading as a self-guidance tool.

If you identify more with auditory learning, don't fret! You can download my Runa Reading app and either read or listen to the information it provides. The app will also allow you to continue down your path of self-discovery long after your thirty-day journey with this book ends.

This book is divided into four parts:

PART I: INTRODUCTION TO THE RUNES

Part I of this book will give you a sense of where the runes came from and how you can use them to enhance your life. First I touch on the mythological ties to the runes, and then I marry ancient insights with my own intuitive ideas about how the runes can be used in modern times. I encourage you to use your own intuition as you explore the runes and decide what resonates with you.

In this part of the book you will experiment with a few different ways to read the runes. You will use the runes for guidance on yes/no questions, and you will establish a daily practice of randomly pulling one rune out of a set of runes to guide you for that day. You will also keep track of your rune pulls on a thirty-day calendar to monitor patterns and answer thought-provoking questions as you go.

In the back of this book, you will see a set of rune cards. To get started, you can cut these cards out and use them for your rune pulls. You can also create or purchase a set of runes. I offer suggestions for making them and recommend various materials you can use based on what appeals to you most. If you prefer digital runes to physical runes, you can download the Rune Read Your Life app and use it for your rune pulls.

I've done extensive research on the runes so I could write this book to be used for practical applications. For a more academic perspective on the runes and Old Norse mythology, I defer to the scholars in the field, some of whom are included in the list of Recommended Reading provided at the end of the book.

PART II: THIRTY DAYS OF PRACTICE

After experimenting with various reading methods and previewing some of the rune passages, you are ready to begin your personal thirty-day transformation. During this process, you will write journal entries that will help you get to know yourself on a deeper level. The lens through which you see the world will shift. Memories, hopes, and distant dreams may come to the surface after lying dormant. For some, this may be a gentle experience; for others, it may create a soul-level awareness that things in your life need to change. Allow whatever it is to emerge. Trust that you can handle anything that comes to light when it arises. At both the subconscious and the superconscious (spiritual) levels, we will learn what we need to when we are meant to learn it.

In this thirty-day period you will also begin to see situations with new clarity and find it easier to understand the intricate interplay of people in your life. It will become easier to see that what you may now consider an unfortunate circumstance is actually a blessing in disguise. There is a lesson in all things. Even the worst storms always pass. In time, regardless of what is blowing up around you, you will find it easier to remain calm, with a deep sense of inner knowledge that a better tomorrow awaits.

You will also understand relationships on a whole new level. Especially for those who challenge you, you will understand how their past and their own unique challenges come into play in their interactions with you, even though you are not responsible for their old wounds. You will learn to identify what is their stuff coming out at you, and you will know not to take it personally. We are all here to learn, and we are each on different legs of our journeys. Accepting that fact without judgement is crucial to our own growth.

Finally, you will develop a practice for setting a daily intention. You will take a few moments to think about the day ahead and decide what energy you want to bring into it. You will declare how you want to show up as a boss, colleague, parent, spouse, or friend. If you wake up with a case of the "mean reds," as Audrey Hepburn said in *Breakfast at Tiffany's*, you can ask for some *wunjo*, or Joy, in your day. Or maybe you have a deadline at work to meet and could benefit from *laguz*, or Flow, to help you get in your zone. Whatever it is you need, there is a rune or combination of runes that can help you set the energetic ball in motion so you can begin your day with complete confidence.

PART III: RUNE MEANINGS

The third part of this book provides a modern interpretation of each rune symbol and offers three "pause and reflect" questions. Here, you have a choice. You can either read about all twenty-five runes in this section and sit with the pause-and-reflect questions symbol by symbol, or you can use this section as a reference to help with your journaling journey in part II. It is up to you.

Either way, I encourage you to take your time with the pause-and-reflect questions in this section. These questions are intended to provoke deeper insight for your consideration and may reveal more than just reading the meanings alone. These questions will provoke you to both look back into your past and to look ahead to better understand what is on your path. If you are verbal, it may help you to talk it out with a trusted friend or counselor. If you are more private and like to write, I recommend that you journal your answers. I advise journaling so you can document your story and have an artifact that describes your spiritual growth as it occurs.

PART IV: MOVING FORWARD

The last part of this book gives suggestions for how to integrate what you have learned about the runes into your daily life.

Some of us dwell in the past. Others have anxiety about the future. In working with the runes, we practice and can master the art of being present. When we are fully present, we live in the moment. We are immersed in whatever we are doing without distraction. We notice little things like the shapes of trees, the warmth of the sun on our cheeks, or the scent of newly blooming spring flowers. We find joy in these little things. When we learn to be fully present, our childlike innocence and happiness returns. Without effort, we easily leave the past in the past and allow the future to naturally unfold without fear or doubt.

The totality of your life today, your childhood, and all the steps in between make up the beautiful tapestry of your story. Write it all down and you will be amazed at the authentic version of you who is waiting to emerge.

If you are using the runes to do readings for other people, you can read them the modern meaning, ask how they would apply the meaning to the area of their life they are asking about, then use the pause-and-reflect questions to advance the conversation. You may notice that as you do readings for others, the messages coming through resonate with you as well. Self-discovery comes in many forms, and by helping others understand themselves, we better understand ourselves.

The runes are a part of who we are today, just as they were a part of us centuries ago. As you will soon experience, the runes will prompt you to explore yourself in a way that is exciting and fun, and they will encourage you to have very different types of conversations with people in your life.

Are you ready for your journey to begin? I'm excited for you and all you are about to experience. Let's go!

PART I

INTRODUCTION TO THE RUNES

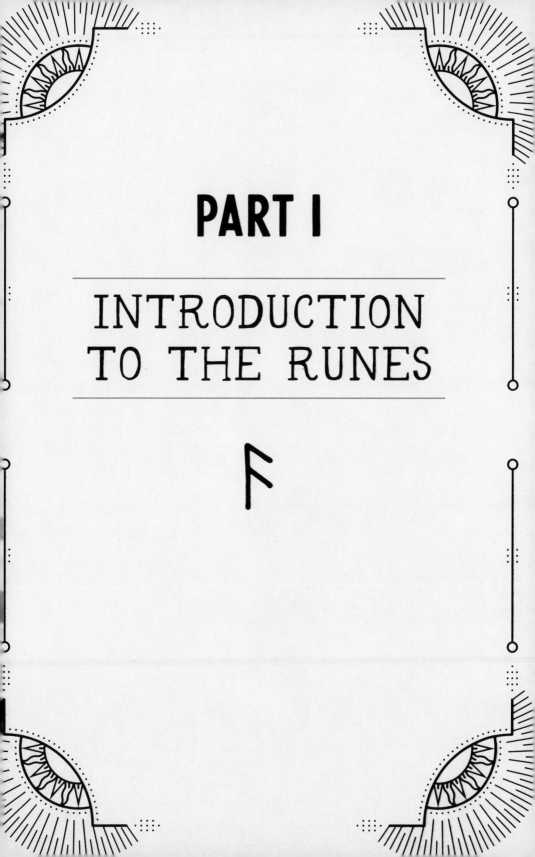

YOUR WORLD
TODAY

I f you were moved to read this book, I already know you. You are a badass, loving superhuman, and I want you to know you are amazing. If you are like me, you try hard every day to do your best to meet the demands of family members, colleagues, friends, and significant others. You pay your bills, clean your home, and keep up with the yard work, and if you are lucky, maybe you find time for a massage once in a while. You are a fixer and the figure-it-out-er who everyone counts on to keep things moving. You have an uncanny ability to multitask. You are both fast and good at doing everything for everyone regardless of whether they ask or not.

Even if we are single, somehow we are in high demand. We fall into bed exhausted each day and tell ourselves, "Maybe tomorrow I will have more free time to get done what I want to do." But our cell phones chime early in the morning, and we leap into lightning-fast action and do-do-do all over again. The world today keeps on spinning faster, expectations on us continue to increase, and somehow we keep rising to the occasion. However . . . to what end? While everyone benefits from our sheer awesomeness, what about us? What is the cost?

As the badass superhumans that we are, we are tired. We have this quiet awareness that we are more stressed than ever before, although we hesitate to admit it. "I can handle it" is what we tell ourselves and others. We spend a lot of time doing our best, yet we sometimes feel defeated, as if all that we give still isn't enough. Current studies suggest that nearly one in ten adults is depressed and that women are twice as likely to be depressed as men. Are we surprised? It's a very different world we are living in now versus the one we entered when we were born.

Our biggest challenges do not stem from our demanding bosses, our cranky coworkers, our impossible-to-please parents, or our occasional high-maintenance friend. It is not really those extra twenty pounds of weight we are carrying on our bodies, or the fact there is a larger-than-life pile of dirty clothes waiting in the laundry room. Our biggest challenge is getting out of our own heads, where we carry on negative self-talk. Our self-doubt creeps in, we feel foggy about what we want and who we are, and then we retreat into ourselves. This process affects our relationship with ourselves and with others. The little voice in our head says things to us that we would never say to anyone else. We move through life staying as busy as we can to drown out the voice.

Maybe we ask for advice from friends or counselors. Maybe we don't. The problem is that we are meant to be most at home and at peace on our insides, rather than having our insides be a place of unrest. The good news is, we can leverage an ancient tool to change that inner narrative from a lecture that makes us feel bad to a melody that lifts us up and makes us feel like the unstoppable, amazing superhumans we truly are.

This ancient tool is the runes, including the symbolic meaning associated with each one. Before explaining what the runes are and describing their rich history, let's begin by exploring the psychology of symbols.

THE PSYCHOLOGY
OF SYMBOLS

S ince the dawn of humanity, symbols have possessed the power to communicate a great deal in one simple character or image. Symbols have been used throughout history to unite people, convey ideas, and telegraph warnings when necessary. Symbols remain as relevant as ever in this digital age, when we want and expect information quickly.

Steve Jobs, the deceased chairman, chief executive officer, and cofounder of Apple, understood this when he cleverly chose to use icons on the iPhone's interactive touch screen. Using icons that were intuitively easy to understand allowed millions of users to adopt this new form of digital communication without needing a user manual. Symbols and icons transcend language barriers and time. Consider the popularity of emojis and how we can change the emotional undertone of a "Hi" text with a smiley face versus a winky face.

Swiss psychoanalyst Carl Jung wrote extensively about how we make subconscious associations based on the symbols we see in the world around us every day. We interpret and analyze symbols without even realizing it, Jung argued in his famous works *Man and His Symbols* and *The Red Book*. He extensively studied myths, art, and iconography from all over the world, which he then drew upon to form a symbolic framework for human psychology that he called the "archetypes." A fascinating result of his research is the Archive for Research in Archetypal Symbolism, which catalogs more than seventeen thousand images and symbols that date back to 3000 BC.

What do symbols do for us? With symbols come emotion and energy. Not only do they have the power to tell us something; they have the innate ability to make us feel something. The ancient Egyptians used an ankh to represent the sun and eternal life. Ankhs were believed to be powerful enough to help the deceased breathe in the afterlife and were therefore placed in tombs. What do you suppose the Egyptians felt when they created copper ankhs for burial rituals? Think of the power in the idea of life after death telegraphed in one symbol.

A six-pointed star called a hexagram, also known as the Star of David in Judaism, is another well-recognized symbol that represents the link between heaven and earth and the union of creation and opposites. This image is not only considered sacred in the Jewish tradition but also to people who study Kabbalah, an ancient spiritual wisdom whose esoteric methods predate world religions. For those who attribute meaning to this symbol, the star evokes divinity and a connection with God.

The ichthys, also referred to as the "Jesus fish," carried an important secret meaning for early Christians. In Greek, ichthys means "fish" and is written as ΙΧΘΥΣ. The secret meaning stems from the fact that, for the Christians, the letters of the Greek word actually form an acrostic—a word in which each letter corresponds to the first letter of another word. Each letter in ΙΧΘΥΣ corresponds to a Greek word in a phrase that, when translated, means "Jesus Christ, Son of God, Savior." Today some Christians proudly display the ichthys bumper sticker as a testament of their faith in Jesus. A college friend of mine had an ichthys tattoo. The symbol instantaneously telegraphs the Christian faith to the world.

These symbols are just a few of thousands that have stood the test of time and whose meaning has remained relatively unchanged. They speak volumes without the need for words. As you are about to discover, rune symbols possess the same power that you can unlock as you journey inward over the next thirty days.

There is a reason why we are inexorably drawn to symbols. Symbols have both universal meaning and personal meaning. When you see an image of a rainbow, what is your immediate association? When I sent a quick poll via text to my Cloud 9 Online meditation app team this morning, the respondents shared the following associations they had with the rainbow image:

Debra: "The rainbow bridge between all of us (here and in heaven)"

Lynne: "Higher dimensions (of spirituality)"

Sabrina: "All colors and cultures coming together"

Brad: "The magic of water meeting light: life and consciousness"

Val: "Gay Pride"

Henry: "Positivity"

When I see a rainbow image, I immediately recall the first movie I ever saw in a movie theater, in 1979 when I was four years old. It was *The Muppet Movie*, and the opening scene was Kermit the Frog singing "The Rainbow Connection" while playing the banjo and sitting on a log in the woods. It was such a magical moment for me, seeing the sights on the big screen and hearing the song's beautifully dreamy and hopeful lyrics and melody. So a rainbow image takes me back to that moment and makes me smile. What do you think of when you see a rainbow symbol?

Symbols help us unlock emotion. When we see a symbol and can make a personal association with it, our rationality is sidestepped. Our roadrunner minds pause from overanalyzing the world around us, and we can drift into a more creative, peaceful place. One simple symbol can help us feel rather than critically think.

When you think about symbols and icons, what images and associations come to mind for you? Draw them in the space below.

What emotional and rational associations do you have with the symbols you've drawn?

_____

_____

_____

_____

_____

_____

And now . . . the fun begins!

HISTORY AND MYTHICAL ROOTS OF THE RUNES

Runes are symbols that constitute an ancient Germanic alphabet dating back centuries. In fact, the word *rune* is derived from the Gothic word *runa,* which means "secret" or "mystery." As such, the runes were used both as a written alphabet for communication and as a divination tool. It was believed that these ancient symbols could help a rune reader anticipate future events and thus avoid unfavorable outcomes.

There are twenty-four runic symbols, each of which corresponds to an English letter or letters and has a Germanic name. Since runes were passed down in the oral tradition, opinions vary regarding how old they actually are. Some texts suggest they date back to 150 AD, while others suggest they are as old as 1200 BC. Variant forms of rune symbols were popular in Nordic Iceland but have also been identified on cave walls. You will find more than one name, form, and meaning for each rune across scholarly texts. Translations, pronunciations, and visual expressions of the runes ebbed and flowed over time. For simplicity's sake, I am presenting you with the names, appearances, and abbreviated meanings I am most drawn to.

For those who are more science-minded, consider the runes as a tool that will trigger a personal association. From a psychologist's point of view, *association* refers to the connections we make in our minds between what we see or hear and prior experiences we've had. This idea of "associationism" extends all the way back to the philosophers Plato and Aristotle, and their early writings on succession of memories. Modern science tells us that our experiences create neural pathways in the brain that trigger how we think, feel, and respond to situations.

For those who favor the mystical, runes are considered a divination tool that connects us with a source of energy and power from beyond our human realm. Today, we would consider this power to come from our guides, guardian angels, higher self, or however we define God.

Most of what we know about the runes today stems from Old Norse mythology captured in a body of medieval poetry known as Eddaic poetry. The runes date back to medieval Scandinavia from the ninth to the thirteenth centuries. The rune set used in this book is known as the elder futhark, so called after the initial sounds in the first six runes in the set's original order *(fehu, uruz, thurisaz, ansuz, raido, kanu)*. These runes served as the predominant alphabet of that time and place before the Latin alphabet took hold across Europe. At the height of their popularity, runes were carved on a variety of surfaces such as jewelry, tools, statues, weapons, and tombs to promote good fortune, bestow protection, or memorialize a person or event. Runes were commonly inscribed on the swords of those going into battle. They were also layered together to create a monogram effect and then used as a "house mark" outside of the home to bless and protect dwellings.

In addition, people used runes to heal common ailments, such as aches and pains or fractures. Runes were also used in midwifery and for healing in general. To deliver healing through the runes, users would inscribe these symbols on personal items, body parts such as the back of the hand, or materials that could be scraped off into liquids to create an elixir that was then consumed.

Finally, runes were used by the *vitki,* individuals versed in rune lore, magic, and healing. During the Viking age in Iceland (ca. 800–1066), the royalty relied upon the *vitki* and runecasting to summon the Norse gods through the runes for prophecy, protection, and fortune.

From a mythological standpoint, the runes were believed to be a gift to us from Odin, the father of all gods. Portrayed in modern films by actors such as Sir Anthony Hopkins in *Thor* and *Thor: Ragnarok,* and voiced by Frank Welker in the animated TV series *Avengers Assemble,* Odin was said to have obtained these magical runic glyphs as a way to tap into archetypal forces. In a perpetual state of learning and eloquent with his words, Odin was called upon for logic, communication, and healing. It was also said that he had ransomed an eye in exchange for cosmic wisdom.

Odin

In Jungian psychology, archetypal forces represent patterns of behavior found in the human condition. To simplify this concept, consider the following. How many of these statements describe someone you know?

"She is such an *angel*."

"He is a real *Casanova*."

"She tends to *mother* everyone."

"She always plays the *victim*."

"He can be such a *martyr*."

"The new boss is the *queen bee*."

These are all examples of archetypes. Through one simple word, we can understand someone's behavioral patterns in certain situations. The Angel archetype exudes a sweet, innocent energy. The Victim archetype vies for sympathy. The Queen archetype has a domineering, controlling energy. The Mother archetype knows best and intervenes even when she isn't asked for help.

So how do archetypes connect to the runes? The runes are divided into three sets of eight, based on the energies that connect the earth and the heavens as represented by three Norse gods: Tyr, Heimdall, and Freya. These three gods have fascinating stories that weave in and out of the stories many of us already know about the more famous gods Thor, Odin, and Loki.

From an archetype standpoint, Odin represents the Leader, Thor the Defender, and Loki the Trickster. We then have Tyr the Warrior, Heimdall the Watcher, and Freya the Goddess. An overview of these godly custodians helps illustrate which archetypal energies are at play when we use the runes for guidance.

Let's begin with the god Tyr. Tyr's eight rune symbols are:

↑ ᛒ ᛖ ᛗ ᛁ ᛚ ᛜ ᛟ ᛝ

Tyr, the son of Odin, is from the Aesir god clan, which is one of the two orginal clans of gods. Tyr is considered the god of justice and lawfulness. The ultimate warrior, he is sometimes called the god of war. Known for his fierceness and courage, Tyr is the god called upon in times of battle. In fact, ↑, which is called *teiwaz,* is a form of Tyr's name, and its one-word meaning is Warrior. Soldiers in Scandinavia would carve this rune symbol into their weapons to evoke the bravery of Tyr.

Tyr looks the part of the ultimate warrior, despite the fact that he is missing a hand. According to myth, Tyr lost his hand to the ferocious wolf Fenrir, one of Loki's monster sons. The myths say that when Fenrir was just a cub, the Aesir permitted the animal to live with them and roam the godly realm, called Asgard. As the wolf grew, the gods became uneasy with the risks associated with his size and strength, and they agreed it was time to shackle Fenrir. However, Fenrir's strength was so great that no chains could hold him. Thus, they enlisted the help of the dwarfs from another realm to create a magical sash that would confine the wolf.

When the gods tried to put this magical sash around the wolf's neck, Fenrir agreed to let them do it, under one condition: one of the gods must place a hand in the wolf's mouth as a demonstration of mutual trust. Without hesistation, the fearless Tyr offered his hand to the wolf. When the sash was placed around Fenrir's neck, its magic took effect, and it began to harden. Fenrir began struggling to get out of the sash, but the more the wolf struggled, the stronger the sash became. Fenrir became increasingly upset, and in retailation, he bit off Tyr's hand. Tyr made his sacrifice in the name of herosim to keep his fellow gods safe. Tyr represents the reality that sometimes bloodshed is necessary to sustain life and well-being. This story teaches us that pain is often a necessary part of growth and the emergence of new possibilities, whether that pain be internal or external, inflicted by the self or by someone else.

As a group, Tyr's eight runes provide *confidence.* Here are the names and meanings of Tyr's runes.

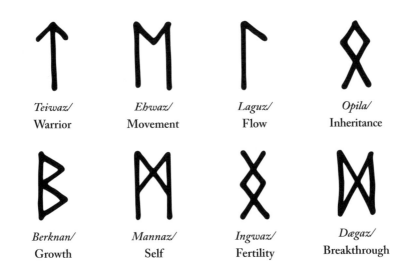

| *Teiwaz/* | *Ehwaz/* | *Laguz/* | *Opila/* |
| Warrior | Movement | Flow | Inheritance |

| *Berknan/* | *Mannaz/* | *Ingwaz/* | *Dægaz/* |
| Growth | Self | Fertility | Breakthrough |

In addition to the Warrior archtype, Tyr possesses the archetypal energies of the Judge, the Protector, and the Avenger. Tyr's eight runes can help you face the most intimidating people and situations. There is an essence of selflessness and sacrifice in Tyr's runes. Tyr doesn't go to battle for the sake of battling; instead, he understands the need for order to protect and preserve the greater good of all the worlds. In today's world, Tyr would be a law enforcement officer, a legislator, or a judge.

Interestingly, the Marvel movies today depict Thor as having many of Tyr's warlike qualities. However, in mythology, Thor was the preferred god of farmers and fishermen, while solidiers invoked the support of Tyr. It seems Hollywood took a few creative freedoms in their depiction of Thor.

Now let's move on to the god Heimdall. Here are Heimdall's eight runes:

Heimdall was a quiet god who also came from the Aesir clan. Heimdall serves as a watchman and guardian of Asgard. He was raised by nine mothers, all of whom were sisters. The gods respected him for his supernaturally powerful sight and hearing, and for his occasional counsel.

A large and holy god, Heimdall sat at the rainbow bridge that connected the gods' realm with the realm of the giants, keeping vigilant watch for any signs of trouble. He never left his post and rarely slept. When he felt that the gods needed to convene, he blew his golden horn, called Gjallarhorn. He had the gift of foreseeing the future and used his horn to warn the gods of Ragnarok, which was the inevitable end of times for the gods.

Heimdall was loyal and faithful. A friend to Thor and foe of Loki, he once advised Thor on how to repossess his hammer, called Mjolnir, from a giant named Thrym. Thrym stole Thor's hammer, which put the gods at risk of possible invasion. Thrym, however, didn't plan to invade Asgard; rather, he desired the beautiful goddess Freya. So he stole Thor's hammer while he slept and held it for the ransom of Freya's hand in marriage.

After Thor and Loki failed to convince Freya to wed the lusty giant, Thor consulted Heimdall for advice. Using his ability to see all and hear all, Heimdall knew when it was best to take swift action, temporarily pause, or do nothing at all. In this situation, he advised Thor to dress up like Freya to deceive Thrym into recovering the hammer. Reluctantly risking his reputation, Thor did as Heimdall suggested. The plan worked, and Thor's hammer was recovered.

As a group, Heimdall's eight runes provide *clarity.* Heimdall's runes are named and defined as follows:

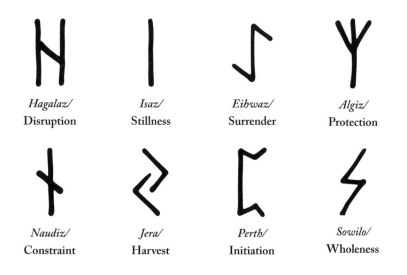

| *Hagalaz/* | *Isaz/* | *Eihwaz/* | *Algiz/* |
| **Disruption** | **Stillness** | **Surrender** | **Protection** |

| *Naudiz/* | *Jera/* | *Perth/* | *Sowilo/* |
| **Constraint** | **Harvest** | **Initiation** | **Wholeness** |

In addition to carrying the archetypal energy of Guardian, Heimdall also carries the archetypes of Visionary, Listener, Hermit, and Counselor. Heimdall is like that best loyal guy friend who is there to listen to you and give advice, and who always keeps your best interests in mind. His eight runes will help you evaluate situations in their purest form so you can gauge how best to respond to situations when they arise.

If you've seen Heimdall portrayed by the actor Idris Elba in the Marvel movies, don't let the scary outfit fool you; Heimdall is a gentle watcher and listener.

Last but not least is our heroine, the beautiful goddess Freya. While the world of mythology is dominated by tales of the male gods, Freya is not to be overlooked. She brings a strong, nurturing archetypal energy to the world.

The strong and beautiful Freya
Illustration by George Peters Designs

Freya's eight rune symbols are the following:

ᚠ ᚢ ᚦ ᚨ ᚱ ᚲ ᚷ ᚹ

Freya is the most prominent goddess in Old Norse mythology. She comes from the Vanir clan of gods, which is significantly smaller than Odin and Thor's Aesir clan. The Vanir gods, as a whole, were considered to be gods of fertility, sexuality, and prosperity. Who doesn't want some of that!

As told in poems and medieval lore, Freya is the goddess of love, beauty, abundance, and destiny. Similar to the Greek goddess Aphrodite, Freya had many admirers and was known as the most beautiful of all goddesses. She is loving and is believed to possess mystical powers used by women who called on her for assistance with matters of the heart and fertility.

Freya is also the deity who embraced the souls of many fallen soldiers. After wars and battles, Freya would journey to the battlefield to bring the souls of the bravest back to heaven, where she would nurture and care for them and their loved ones for the rest of eternity. Thus, in addition to her ties to life and love, Freya also has ties to death and battle. In this we see traces of the Egyptian goddess Isis, who represented both heaven and hell, and the Greek goddess Persephone, who spent half her time in the dark underworld.

Many desired Freya, but she was married to the god Od (not to be confused with Odin), who traveled often, leaving her alone for long periods of time. In his absence, she was lavished with attention and gifts from her many admirers, which provided her with fleeting pleasure. However, the high of temporary joy would quickly fade, leaving Freya feeling lost and melancholy. She was said to cry tears of rose gold for Od as she wandered the lands searching for him.

Freya's beauty was a source of power for her, but with it came a burden. While most felt immense love for Freya, her beauty and power provoked jealousy and cruelty from some, who portrayed her as promiscuous and hedonistic. While many ancient texts refer to this, my belief is that she was misrepresented by Loki and other males who felt threatened by the inherent power that comes with beauty, warmth, and grace.

As a group, Freya's eight symbols tie to *love* and *relationships*. Here are Freya's runes with their names and meanings:

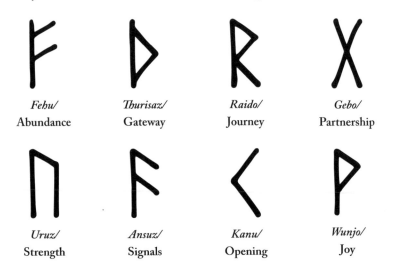

Fehu/ Abundance	*Thurisaz/* Gateway	*Raido/* Journey	*Gebo/* Partnership
Uruz/ Strength	*Ansuz/* Signals	*Kanu/* Opening	*Wunjo/* Joy

When you read the one-word meanings of these eight runes, Freya's complex story comes to life, as do its associated archetypal forces. Freya's eight runes can help guide you when it comes to matters of the heart. In addition to possessing the sensual Goddess energetic archetype, Freya emits the archetypal energies of Angel, Mother, Rescuer, Mystic, and Companion.

I consider Freya to be the goddesses' goddess as she represents our love of others, and just as important, our love for *ourselves*.

The table below summarizes the relationships between the gods, the runes, and the archetypes.

	TYR	HEIMDALL	FREYA
Collective Energy	Confidence	Clarity	Love and relationships
Archetypes	Warrior, Judge, Protector, Avenger	Guardian, Visionary, Listener, Hermit, Counselor	Goddess, Angel, Mother, Rescuer, Mystic, Companion
Rune Meanings	Warrior, Growth, Movement, Self, Flow, Fertility, Inheritance, Breakthrough	Disruption, Constraint, Stillness, Harvest, Surrender, Initiation, Protection, Wholeness	Abundance, Strength, Gateway, Signals, Journey, Opening, Partnership, Joy
Rune Symbols	↑ᛒᛗᛗᚷᛉᛃᛞ	ᚺᛏᛁᛇᛃᚲᛦᛉ	ᚠᚢᚦᚨᚱᚲᚷᛈ

RUNES IN THE
WORLD TODAY

n the present day, the runes have a very small following. Runes are no longer used as an alphabet but instead as a means of divine communication and a manifestation tool for influencing outcomes through what some call the Law of Attraction. The Law of Attraction is the principle that you can draw in positive things by focusing on and expecting positive things. Conversely, you can also draw in negative things by focusing on and expecting negative things. You get back from the universe what you put out to the universe.

For example, the rune symbol ᛜ *ingwaz* represents fertility, family, and sexual energy. It could be used to inspire continuity and connection. Some may use it to literally aid in a pregnancy. Regardless of the historical meaning of *ingwaz*, if we believe it has the power to aid in fertility, so it will be.

Given my desire to create fertile ground in every business development conversation I have, I chose to use *ingwaz* in a logo for one of my companies, Experience Design International (EDI). How this came to be is an interesting story. As I was writing up a creative brief for my graphic designers Adnan and Ahsan, who were tasked with creating my new logo, I had a strong feeling we needed a shape or icon incorporated into the

EDI logo. Any time I have a feeling about something, I always honor it and activate my intuitive listening skill.

Whenever I want to tap in to my inner source for divine guidance, I close my eyes and ask my question. Often, I will see an image or get an immediate answer in my mind. So, with eyes closed, I started by asking, "Is there to be a shape in the Experience Design International logo?" In my mind's eye, I immediately saw a giant black *Y*, which in my own internal system means *yes*. I then asked, "Will you show me the symbol?" and I immediately saw ᛉ. I thought, "Cool! It's a rune!" And how perfect that it signifies fertility.

But, being a researcher at heart, I often like a second form of validation. I reached for my bag of runes, held them with my eyes closed, and said, "Show me if a rune symbol should be part of the Experience Design International logo. If there is to be no symbol, I will draw the blank rune."

Guess what happened? I drew ᛉ on the first try! I can't even tell you I was surprised, since I am so connected to the runes at this point. I just laughed out loud and said, "Of course! Thank you!" I was, and remain, so grateful that I have the runes as a part of my self-guidance system. And so, the logo was born.

Thankfully, my business partner, Henry, is a good sport and left the artistic execution up to me. Since Henry grew up in Syracuse, New York, I instructed our graphic designers to use the Pantone colors from the Syracuse University logo, which include the deep orange and dark gray that are now part of our logo. In doing this, I was blending together my love of runes with Henry's love of his hometown roots.

By November 2017, nine months after its formation, the business was thriving. We achieved a sales milestone assuring us that what we had launched would achieve sustained success. The nine-month mark for me is an interesting parallel to an actual pregnancy. EDI needed nine full months to grow and mature. In those first several months, we were hopeful and optimistic, but we weren't completely sure we would hit our sales goals by the end of 2017. However, we signed our first large international account, and from that moment forward more and more business continued to flow to EDI. I am positive that the energy of the *ingwaz* symbol in our logo contributes to our success.

It doesn't matter whether you are drawn to the more science-based explanation of the runes or the more mystical, energy-based explanation. Incorporating runes into your daily routine is a way to be more mindful and set a daily intention into action. Runes provide us with a fun methodology for having a dialogue with our inner selves so we can live life while being as fully aware and awake as possible. The more we trust the runes as a source of wisdom and as an accelerator for connecting with our true selves, the more powerful our connection becomes to our higher source that knows all. The key is to make it a habit throughout your day to pause and ask the questions you need to make the best decisions possible that will move you in the direction you really want to go.

You may find over time that you no longer need a physical set of runes. Nowadays, I can close my eyes, ask any question, and see a rune symbol or series of symbols in my mind without needing my bag of runes. If you begin working with the runes regularly, this will very likely be a skill you effortlessly develop too.

FIRST IMPRESSIONS

Before further exposure to the runes and their modern meanings, let's begin by capturing your first impressions of what each symbol means to you. On the following pages, you will be exposed to three different runes. This exercise is all about your gut-instinct association with each rune, so the less you know about the runes, the better.

Take a moment to examine each of the following runes in this exercise. Close your eyes and visualize each symbol in your mind. If you have a hard time seeing the symbol, imagine you are drawing the symbol on a chalkboard or in the sand on the beach. Record words, phrases, feelings, and images that surface as you sit with each rune.

Ready?

What words or phrases come to mind when you see this symbol?
Perhaps you sense a letter. Record your first impression.

_____

_____

_____

_____

_____

_____

_____

If you close your eyes and visualize this symbol, what do you feel
when you imagine it?

_____

_____

_____

_____

_____

_____

_____

This rune is called *thurisaz,* which means Gateway. Take a moment and sit with the word Gateway in your mind. What images do you see? Draw a picture of what you see:

Let's try another rune and explore what associations you have with the symbol. What words or phrases come to mind when you see this symbol?

_____

_____

_____

_____

_____

_____

If you close your eyes and visualize it, what do you feel?

_____

_____

_____

_____

_____

_____

This rune is called *mannaz,* which means the Self. Take a moment and sit with the phrase "the Self" in your mind. What images do you see? Draw a picture of what you see:

Let's try one last rune before you see the entire set of rune symbols. What words or phrases come to mind when you see this symbol?

_____

_____

_____

_____

_____

_____

If you close your eyes and visualize it, what do you feel?

_____

_____

_____

_____

_____

This rune is called *opila*, which means Inheritance. Take a moment and sit with the word Inheritance in your mind. What images do you see? Draw a picture of what you see:

Now flip to part II of this book and look up the modern meanings of *thurisaz, mannaz,* and *opila.* Then, in your own words, describe the meaning of each rune. How does this compare to what you wrote?

ᚦ	ᛗ	ᛟ
THURISAZ	*MANNAZ*	*OPILA*

Now let's study an illustration of the full set of runes.

SUMMARY OF RUNE SYMBOLS

The illustration below depicts the twenty-four runes in the elder futhark. Over time, this alphabet grew to twenty-seven and then thirty-one characters. When we work with the runes today, however, it is most common to use the original set of twenty-four plus one blank rune that is optional based on personal preference.

Take a moment to evaluate each symbol. Which symbol or symbols are you drawn to most? Why? Do any of them feel familiar to you? Draw them in the space below and note what drew you in about the symbol or symbols you chose.

Now, in part III of this book, look up the meaning of the rune or runes you drew above. How does the meaning apply to your life right now? Journal your observations below.

Some of the rune symbols may feel familiar based on images we see in the world today. If you are athletically inclined, you may have heard of a race called the Ragnar Relay Series, a set of long-distance relay races that take place in the United States. The Ragnar Relays consist of a twenty-four-hour, two-hundred-mile city-to-city race run by teams of six to twelve runners. If you've had the opportunity to run in this race, you know inevitably you will end up running a five-mile (or more) leg of the race between nine p.m. and five a.m. wearing a headlamp in the pitch blackness of night. It is downright spooky running at night, even with your team van following you! They say the body only requires five hours of rest to fully recover from physically strenuous activity such as a mid-distance run, and this race proves it.

Now let's examine the Ragnar logo. If you look closely at the logo and compare it to the runes on the prior page, what two runes do you see? If you are unfamiliar with this logo, take a moment to google it.

What about the Nike logo? Turned on its side, which rune does it resemble?

In the Ragnar logo, can you see Protection ᛉ and Journey ᚱ? These are such perfect symbols for this race, in which you take an epic two-hundred-mile journey by foot. Indeed, any runner—day or night—could always use a little protection against injury or accident when running on unfamiliar landscapes. In the Nike logo, can you see Flow ᛚ? What athlete wouldn't want to be in their flow zone when training and getting fit?

Did the brilliant marketing minds behind these brands intentionally leverage the powers of the runes? Maybe. Maybe not. I personally believe whether we have learned about them in this lifetime or not, we will find they are familiar to us because on a cellular and soul level, we have seen them before. We do know them and may actually be remembering them from past lifetimes.

TUNING INTO THE RUNES' MESSAGES

We all have the ability to hear our inner wisdom speak, even if we are not initiating the dialogue. The moment we express an outward interest in the runes, it is as if we energetically activate a live connection with the symbols. When we do this, we are tuning into their unique frequencies, and with each frequency comes a higher level of guidance, both when we ask for it as well as when we least expect it.

I collected my first set of rune stones on the Connecticut shore on October 13, 2014. I didn't realize it at the time, but that date would have been my mother's sixtieth birthday. I combed the beach and chose twenty-five flat ocean stones with care. It was a very relaxing and introspective experience. The beach is my favorite place to go when I need to rest and recharge, so the idea of stones from the ocean gives me an immediate sense of relaxation and floods me with happy memories.

I brought the stones home and didn't do anything with them for exactly 365 days. I can't really explain why. I just wasn't moved to do anything for an entire year. Again, without being consciously aware of the date, I woke up on October 13, 2015, with an overwhelming sense that I needed to spend the day alone.

I went out for a hike and then felt the urge to go buy my first book on reading runes. I sat down in the bookstore with a hot cup of coffee and stared at the rune symbols. I looked at the one-word meaning of each, and within minutes, I knew them all. It felt as if I was remembering them, even though I was seeing them for the first time.

After reading most of the book, I felt compelled to go to the craft store to buy paint so I could create and charge my first set of rune stones. I needed to do so that day. Charging an object simply means creating a personal connection with it, such as when a child first receives a teddy bear and hugs it, forming an immediate bond with the object. For me, painting a rune on each stone while focusing on the meaning of each symbol was my way of charging the stones with my energy.

It wasn't until I returned home and was hand-painting them that I realized the date: it was Mom's birthday again. I smiled and thought to myself, "Mom, it feels like we just spent the entire day together, and today has been a great day!"

I used that first set of runes for nearly a year. I had them with me at all times. Any time I felt moved to pull a rune stone, I did. Eventually, I began pulling runes for others. Sometimes they would be people I knew, and other times they were perfect strangers.

Admittedly, it was awkward at first. But what I quickly realized was this: all I had to do was ask someone to think about an area of her life in which she needed guidance, then pull a rune and share the meaning. The person then connected what I said to her situation and explained to me the personal meaning she derived.

The runes were like my security blanket that I always carried with me. Somehow, just knowing they were near gave me a sense of comfort. Eventually the day came when I put my hand in the little velvet bag in which I kept them and felt that something was off. I poured the runes out and discovered that several of my rune stones had inexplicably crumbled.

At first, I looked for a rational explanation: Did I drop the bag on a hard surface? Did something heavy crush them? Since the runes were in my larger bag that held my laptop, I could easily rule out something large damaging the runes, since my laptop was intact. I closed my eyes and asked the question, "What is the significance of these runes crumbling?"

An answer immediately popped into my mind: "You are meant to make new ones."

Okay, got it.

Now that I'd learned a little about stones from the sea, I decided I needed to collect new stones that were denser and less sediment-based. As it turned out, I was now consulting a few days a week for a company in Rhode Island, so on my business trips I would leave my hotel at sunrise and walk on Narragansett Beach looking for flat, black rocks that I knew to be harder than the stones I'd collected from the Connecticut shore.

The act of looking for little black sea stones was a special experience. I would walk and fill my pockets. At one point, I felt equally drawn to flat white stones as well, so my left pocket held white stones while my right pocket held black stones.

After collecting more than one hundred stones, I felt satisfied enough to move to the next phase and paint my new set. It felt important to collect and choose every stone. In doing so, I created a memory and what felt like an immediate bond with the stones.

Interestingly, I painted and charged three sets for others before painting a set for myself. Creating rune stones for others and teaching people about them was part of what I needed to do.

A funny thing happens once you develop a connection to rune symbols. You begin noticing them everywhere. You also may receive intuitive messages when you see symbols out in the world. The most significant experience I had like this occurred on one of my final days in Rhode Island. Although my stone-collecting efforts were complete, I noticed a white sea stone with a natural marking on it that was the same as ᚼ, *hagalaz,* the runic symbol for Disruption. It was so striking that I picked it up, took a picture of it, and posted it on Facebook, noting that it represented Disruption. I wondered what would happen next. Here is what I posted:

Delanea Davis is in Narragansett, Rhode Island.
May 27, 2016 ·

Just found this stone on the beach that naturally has the Runic symbol called "Hagalaz" which represents "disruption". I've been pulling it & seeing it a lot lately in my Runes readings. I love how patterns reoccur over and over until the delivered message is fully received.

When the runic symbol for Disruption appears, it indicates the coming of an event that has the potential to turn things upside down, with inevitable damage done. However, the greater the disruptive force, the greater the potential for growth and rebirth on the other side when things settle back down. I started my day very curious about which shoe might drop in my life.

Three hours later, I was working in a coffee shop near my client's business operation. The client was a visionary CEO who had invested his life savings in his company and worked tirelessly around the clock to make his dream succeed. This CEO came barreling into the coffee shop to find me and said, "Pack up your things. We need to leave *right now.*"

I said, "Is everything okay?"

"There's no time to talk. We need to leave immediately."

"Okay," I said, "but where are we going?"

"To Providence. The FBI has a warrant out for my arrest."

Say *what?* Talk about worlds turning upside down!

The car ride to Providence was surreal. I drove as the CEO chain-smoked and filled me in on the trouble he'd gotten himself into. He was being charged with multiple felonies, and he'd hired a defense attorney in anticipation of imminent trouble. Today was the day it was all going down. In addition to the FBI, the district attorney for the city of Providence was now involved too.

The days that followed were a whirlwind. My business partner, Rita, jumped in to assist with a very harrowing and emotional situation. In a matter of hours, we had to act fast and assemble a cross-functional crisis management team: crisis communication support, social support for the CEO's family, attorneys, risk-management advisors—very expensive "paid friends," I'll call them. You learn to bond fast when the meter is running with a cast like that.

This occurred on the Friday of Memorial Day weekend, and the DA's office was giving the CEO until Tuesday to turn himself in. So we had three days to prepare for what might have created a national news media frenzy. The best-case scenario was for the story to remain contained to state newspapers and TV. Either way, approximately twenty investors needed to be notified, an employee plan needed to be activated, and the family and extended family of the CEO needed some level of communication. And there I was in the middle of all of it.

It was the most intense professional experience I have ever had, not to mention emotionally harrowing, as the CEO had been a close family friend for many years. I actually gave the white Disruption stone to the CEO in the midst of all of this and told him I found it on the beach the day all of this broke. At one point he broke down and cried to Rita and me, confessing that years ago, a psychic intuitive had told him that when he was about forty years old he would be sentenced to prison and lose his family. She'd provided details that exactly matched what was playing out now.

"I should have heeded her warning," he said while crying to us. "I had a chance to make different choices, but I didn't. Why didn't I listen?"

There was nothing we could do to influence what would happen next. Nor was there much either of us could say to console him. After nearly a year under house arrest, the CEO was sentenced to one year and one day in prison on a reduced charge. Many of us are given both gentle and severe warnings but stay on our current path anyway. From pain and suffering come our greatest learning.

You might think this would have scared me away from runes, but the reality is, my attraction to the runes transformed from intrigue to respect.

Ironically, seven months prior to the CEO's arrest I had given him a rune reading that contained a very clear warning. I had pulled three runes for him on October 28, 2015, and sent him the rune reading in an email. Using *The Book of Runes* by Ralph Blum as my guide, I offered the following reading:

> **Current Situation:** ᛗ *Mannaz* representing the Self. Everything begins with you. Only clarity and a willingness to change are effective now. Be mindful of what is coming to be and passing away. This is a time of growth and rectification for you, which is critical for progress. Be in this world, but not completely of it. Be open and receptive to the messages they are sending to you. Be as present as possible and do each task because it's what you love to do. Take care not to be clouded by the idea of merit and accomplishment.

Obstacle to Overcome: ᛇ *Eihwaz* representing Surrender. When an obstacle appears in our path, our tendency is to force it away or defeat it. However, the higher-level perspective is sometimes a delay or something going off track, which can actually be beneficial. Overeagerness or impatience can work against you. Consider the consequences of your actions before you act, so you can avert difficult situations via the right actions. Through difficulty and inconvenience comes growth. You are being asked to let things flow and to acknowledge a setback as a setback. Things will become effortless once you give into the natural order in which all things move.

Resolution: ᛚ *Laguz* but inverted, representing the opposite of Flow. You are being cautioned against trying to exceed your own strength and excessive striving. It is critical that you draw on your own instincts to keep you in balance. You are being asked to go within and honor your receptive side.

Wrap Up: Just "be," don't always "do." Periods of stillness will help you recharge to go faster later. Give yourself permission to have unplanned days of nothing when the need arises. While this is against your nature, honor it when something is freezing you. Attempting to push through it and "get shit done" could result in hasty decisions that are better left for a day with a clear, fresh head. Don't work against yourself. Allow your Higher Self to drive when he steps in. Your body and mind are simply catching up to where your higher-level consciousness is.

I pulled runes for him a few times after that, and ᛚ, *laguz*, would appear inverted again and again. This CEO pushed himself to his own breaking point, and I believe deep down he knew the spiral would consume him. His Higher Self was speaking to him through the runes, but his human side was unwilling to listen. This is the struggle we all have from time to time when our gut is trying to get through to our heads. The runes simply bridge the conversation between our head (our Human Self), which can be mired in fear and ego, and our gut (our Higher Self), which is all-knowing and always has our highest and greatest good in perspective.

It is helpful to journal about the messages you receive, as you can see from the story I just shared. Sometimes we cannot hear or execute on a message when we are first given it, but we may feel appropriately motivated to so do at a later date.

THINGS TO NOTE ABOUT THE RUNES

There are a few rune symbols that resemble each other. You may want to examine them closely so you correctly identify them when you are doing your rune readings.

Let's begin with X, which is *gebo*, Partnership, and ᛉ, which is *naudiz*, Constraint. Notice that the *gebo* is a symmetrical character, forming a perfectly balanced X. Notice that in *naudiz* the lines are asymmetrical, and the symbol is slightly askew.

Two more runes that look similar are ᛋ, *sowilo*, Wholeness, and ᛇ, *eihwaz*, Surrender. Notice that *sowilo* somewhat resembles an *S* and points slightly upward, while *eihwaz* resembles a *z* and points slightly downward. Before you create your runes, you may want to practice drawing each of these sets of symbols so you can draw them in a way that is clearly differentiated and read them accordingly. You may also see *sowilo* appear this way in some texts: ᚴ.

I also want to draw your attention to ᛜ, *ingwaz*, Fertility. I am personally drawn to this depiction of the symbol: ᛜ. However, some depict *ingwaz* as ◊. If you buy premade runes, *ingwaz* may be represented either way.

You will also notice in the prior table that in addition to twenty-four symbols there is a line that represents the Unknown and is a blank rune. Some use the blank when reading runes, while others do not. I personally like the blank and find it rarely comes up. The blank rune represents the idea that some things are beyond our present-day understanding, are not yet to be known, or cannot be foreseen. This idea resonates with me, so I choose to incorporate a blank rune into my sets. Go with what intuitively feels right for you. I have also seen ◊ used to represent the blank rune in some commercially sold rune sets.

If a rune is pulled or cast upside down, many traditional rune readers consider it "merkstave," which suggests the rune has an alternate, dark meaning. Because I believe that all divine guidance comes from a place of pure love and light, the idea of an alternate "dark" meaning does not sit well with me from both a scientific and a spiritual standpoint.

Since the goal of using the runes is to develop clarity and confidence, a menacing message is not what we need to ease our minds and help us understand the steps we need to take to move forward on our journey. Our spirit guides and Higher Self speak to us like a precious child, using language that makes us feel infinitely supported and loved. We should only come away from these intimate conversations feeling inspired and cherished, even if we are being encouraged to take a step that scares us a little. When rune symbols appear to me intuitively in my mind's eye, I usually see them right-side up.

For these reasons, I do not offer an entirely different interpretation for a rune cast upside down. To me, seeing a rune upside down could be simply interpreted as your tendency to want to resist the advice that the rune is offering. It is as if the rune is saying, "You may not like hearing this now, but. . . ." because you may be dismissive of the advice you are getting.

To this end, I suggest that you memorize how each rune should appear when it is pulled or cast right-side up so you can recognize when it is sideways or upside down. For runes that are symmetrical in nature, there is no inversion. *Gebo*, for example, appears like this X right-side up, and this ⋈ when turned on its side. *Ingwaz* is another that maintains its symmetry when right-side up, turned on its side, or upside down: ⋈ versus ⋈.

Sowilo is an interesting one, as I have seen it appear as ⚡ and ⋏. Both are considered right-side up, so to speak.

Over time, you may develop your own level of interpretation of why a rune may appear merkstave. Go by what feels right to you when it comes to this. There is no wrong method. You are creating your own system for accessing this higher-level guidance.

DRAWING THE RUNES TO PRACTICE AND RELAX

In grade school, when we were learning to read and write, we began by drawing each letter. I find drawing the runes very calming. In the rare moments when I feel anxious about something, I doodle combinations of runes; I find this produces the same effect as meditating, which makes me relax completely.

Using the watermark below, take a few minutes to trace each rune. Pay attention to how you feel as you do this. Begin by tracing the runes you are drawn to most.

ESTABLISHING RUNE RITUALS

Personal rituals are a part of everyday life. We have a morning ritual that may include coffee and reading the latest events on social media before we start our day. We may have a ritual for how and when we like to work out. Even when we prepare for bed, we engage in habitual practices. Working with the runes is no different. I would like you to consider creating your own rituals around the following rune-related tasks:

- selecting your first rune set
- charging your runes
- storing your runes
- clearing and charging your runes

Let's start with selecting your runes. Choosing the right runes for you is an important part of the process. The more connected you feel to your set, the more likely you are to incorporate them into your life.

Begin by considering which material you are drawn to. Runes can be created on any flat surface. Following are a few common basic rune materials:

- stones—from the ocean, a river, the earth, or any place that has significance to you
- metal—in the form of a pressed or etched coin
- wood—from any variety of trees, cut from a thin branch into small discs
- clay—which you can make and bake yourself
- crystals—polished or tumbled, set in any color or crystal type

Next, decide if you want to create them on your own or buy a premade set. I have a strong personal bias toward making them myself. The more personalized your runes, the deeper your connection to them will be. If you decide to make them, you can either buy your base material or collect your own before inscribing it.

If you collect your own material, stones, wood, and clay all make great base material for runes. If you use stones, you can etch them with a Dremel or paint the runes on them. If you use wood, you can carve them or use a wood-burning tool. If you use clay, you can also carve them or paint the runes on them.

If you prefer to buy your base material, you can order a set of twenty-five plain clay poker chips online, along with an oil-based paint pen, and you can use the paint pen to draw each rune on a poker chip. This simple ten-minute DIY method, which I use in my rune workshops, saves a lot of time.

Here is an example of a full set of runes drawn on clay chips:

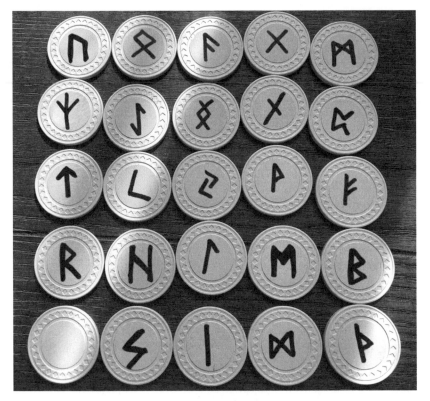

Runes on clay poker chips

You can also visit your local craft store. My artist friend Sabrina created her first set of runes using multicolored glass chips. Here is her set:

Runes on glass

If you prefer higher-quality materials, a great place to visit is Pelham Greyson, a large stone and crystal retailer and wholesaler in North Stonington, Connecticut. If you are not in the area, you can visit them online at www.pelhamgrayson.com and look at their selection of tumbled gemstones. Flattened, polished stones are ideal for runes. Note that the larger you go in size, the more delicate the stones will be.

If you choose polished crystals as your base material, select stones that are about the size of a nickel. If they are larger than the size of a quarter, they shatter easily if dropped or cast on a hard surface.

I recently made two sets using polished crystals that I obtained from Pelham Greyson. Selecting crystals as a base for the runes is an experience in and of itself! My most recently created rune stones appear below. They were about one and a half inches long . . . and chipped! Smaller is better with this rune base.

The purple amethyst is known to soothe and relax. It inspires both creativity and logic, which are a great frequencies to tap into when reading the runes. Black agate is known to increase concentration and focus. It connects the mind with the spirit while keeping you grounded, which is also a great foundation when reading the runes.

Runes on purple amethyst

Runes on black agate

I have experimented with several methods of etching runes in many surfaces. For ease of use, I recommend buying fine-point oil-based paint pens for inscribing your runes, regardless of the type of base material you use. White paint appears particularly brilliant on dark stones and crystals, although paint pens come in many colors. After applying the rune symbols, finish with a clear protective coat such as an acrylic spray found at your local craft store.

If creating your own set of runes is not your thing, you can buy them online or at most metaphysical shops. Depending on the material, they can range in price from $10 to $50 per set. I personally love rose quartz as a base material. Rose quartz, known as the stone of the heart, provides peace, compassion, and healing, effects that are felt powerfully when runes are etched into the stones. The most expensive set of premade runes I've seen was at a metaphysical shop in Denver. The runes were hand cut and carved into birchwood for $80.

Now let's move on to charging your runes. If you elected to make your own runes, you'll already have a connection to the material and the symbols. However, it is important that you take steps to charge them to deepen your connection to them and activate your access to the higher-level wisdom you seek through them.

There is no one way to do this, but here are a few ideas. I personally use all of the following methods:

- Lay all the runes out on a table, face up. One by one, pick up each rune and hold it in your hand while you look up its name and description. Say aloud, for example, "This is the rune called *ansuz,* which corresponds to the letter *A.* When I pull this rune, I will interpret it to mean . . . ." Then read the rune description aloud. Highlight or underline words or phrases in the passage that resonate most with you. When you feel ready, move on to the next rune. Do this until all twenty-four runes are charged.

- Sleep with the runes under your pillow for three days. Set the intention that, by keeping them under your pillow, you are unlocking the ancient wisdom that the runes bring, and you are energetically tying each rune in your set to you.

- Use them daily, and keep them with you everywhere you go.

While some may question the importance of charging your runes, I would say it's all what you make of it. If you are reading this book, you are intuitively drawn to the runes and already have a relationship with the symbols. As I mentioned, after I reviewed the symbols and their one-word meanings for the first time, I knew them all almost immediately, and I do not have a photographic memory. I expect this will happen for you too.

Here is a fun tip: look at the runes and their meanings before taking a nap or going to bed. Research shows our memory capacity is heightened if we review things just before we sleep.

When it comes to storing and transporting your runes, you can opt for something more traditional, such as a drawstring pouch, which works well. Others may feel drawn to keep their runes stored in a glass or wooden box that is kept safely at home. In my first few years of working with the runes, I wanted to always keep them with me because I felt they were an extension of me, so I kept them in a hand-sewn drawstring bag that my friend Gina brought me back from a trip she had taken to China.

Now I have several sets of runes made of various materials all over my home. They are in my plants, hanging as carved ornaments, on display on my mantel—pretty much everywhere.

Some people choose to keep their runes wrapped in a special cloth that they open and use as a place mat of sorts onto which they cast the runes ceremonially. I do not do this, but if you feel drawn to do it, by all means do so.

The key is to create your own customs and traditions around how you want to store your runes, such as whether they will be mobile or stationary and whether you feel guided to set a special "stage" upon which to read, so to speak.

Finally, you may elect to have a cleaning and clearing practice for your runes. If you believe objects can be influenced by energetic vibrations, just as we humans can, you may want to establish a way to clear your rune stones after working with them. Clearing them is a way to dissipate stagnant or unpleasant energy that your runes may absorb over time. Think of it like putting new batteries in an electronic device. By clearing and cleaning the runes, we amplify the power they hold for us.

Here are a few methods for clearing, cleaning, and recharging your runes:

- Lay your runes out with the symbols facing up. Close your eyes and visualize each rune as being washed by pure, white, brilliant light. Hold this image in your mind for a few moments, and set the intention in your mind that this white, healing light is clearing and cleaning your runes.

- Hold a few runes at a time in your hands under running water. Imagine the cool water washing away any energetic debris that may be attached to them.

- Set your runes either in a windowsill or outside where they can be exposed to direct sunlight or moonlight. Allow the naturally restorative power of the sun or moon to reset and recharge your runes.

- Burn dried sage, and direct the smoke toward your runes. State the intention either aloud or in your mind that you are cleaning and clearing them.

Note that you can use all of these rituals, some of them, or none of them at your discretion. You can even create your own rituals. You may decide you are the only person who can touch your runes, or you may allow anyone to touch them. You may choose to sleep with them in a special place. Do whatever feels right to you. There is no wrong method here, because it is the energy and intention behind what you do that creates the magic between you and your runes.

GETTING STARTED: ACTIVATING AND PRACTICING RUNE READINGS

Before we dive into reading the runes, let's activate your connection with the runes by helping you become more familiar with them as an alphabet.

Take a moment and look at the phrases below spelled out in runic symbols. Can you interpret any of the words intuitively before decoding them? These letters may feel inexplicably familiar to you.

What do you sense? When you are ready, use the Index of Runes that appear at the beginning of Part III to decode these phrases.

ᚲᚠᚱᚲᛗ ᛗᛁᛗᚨ

_____

_____

_____

_____

ᛟᚲᛗᚻ ᛌᛟᚢᚱ ᚻᛗᚠᚱᛏ

_____

_____

_____

_____

Looking again at the full rune alphabet, are there any symbols to which you feel particularly drawn? Write them in the space below.

Take a moment to look up the meaning of those rune symbols. Do any of their meanings personally resonate with you? Why? Record your thoughts below.

_____

_____

_____

_____

_____

_____

Now, let's create your runic monogram. Transcribe the first, middle, and last initials of your name in rune symbols.

My initials are D. A. D. In runes, my monogram would be:

This monogram is *dægaz-ansuz-dægaz,* which means Breakthrough-Signals-Breakthrough. When I consider how this relates to the big picture of my life, I would say that my life story is about a series of challenges that I have faced and overcome, leveling up each time. The more I am aware of and receptive to the signals and guidance I am being given all the time, the easier it has become to persevere. The more open I become, the more grateful I am to my life-changing *aha* moments.

While I wasn't always aware of it, I have been mentored all my life by guides that exist in both human form and in spiritual form. They have sent me intuitive signals all along. One crucial guide is my mom. She is around me all the time and provides a special level of support when it comes to matters of the heart, despite the fact that she transitioned from human form to spiritual form when I was twenty-three years old.

After she passed, she began sending me signals that she was around. She had clever ways of getting my attention, especially when she felt I was off my path. Her go-to move was to blow out light bulbs in my house. Four, five, and six light bulbs would blow out within a week. It took me awhile to discern this unusual pattern. I eventually realized this would happen at times in my life when I felt like things were spinning out of control—times when I felt lost, when I felt I wasn't living my life as honestly and authentically as I needed to. It was in those moments when I needed Mom's advice the most.

It wasn't until I was thirty-five years old that I would start talking to my mom in times of utter desperation. I would tearfully ask, "Mom, I need your help. What would you tell me to do?" Somehow I would instantly know what she would say. I could almost hear her practical yet supportive advice in my mind. I came to realize that she is always there and can help facilitate any breakthrough I need, no matter how big or small the challenge.

Now, years later, I am open to receiving the signals from anyone, anywhere, anytime. As a result, the breakthroughs come more frequently without all the pain that can often accompany them.

With your own life story in mind, how would you summarize your life story based on your initials in rune symbols?

Capture your story in writing.

_____

_____

_____

_____

_____

_____

These symbol association exercises serve as practice for how you will work with the runes while you develop your relationship with them. When you pull runes, you will access both sides of your brain. You will access your left brain to help you think in words, recall facts, and apply logic. You will also draw upon your right brain, which enables you to visualize, imagine, and activate your intuition. When we leverage both sides of our brain in this fashion, we attain new levels of clarity and confidence.

Now let's practice various methods for reading the runes, starting with reading runes for yourself.

RUNES FOR
GUIDING THE SELF

think of runes like a dynamic personal GPS that is always on and ready to give direction at any time. While you will derive a benefit if you use them sporadically, it is best to incorporate them into your life by establishing a daily practice. You can use runes to set the focus of your day or at the close of the day before bed. You can also use them as questions come up throughout your day.

Having a set of runes serves to remind us to pause before we react or jump to a conclusion. For many of us, life moves at warp speed, and it is easy to fall into the "ready-fire-aim" trap in our personal and professional lives. That said, keeping your runes in a standard place—like on your nightstand, on your desk at work, or in your backpack—is a way to remember to use them for more clarity and calm in your life.

When using the runes to guide yourself, you can ask either specific or broad questions. You can ask simple yes-or-no questions, or you can ask higher-level questions, like "What do I need to know about this situation?" You can ask for guidance on how to handle a difficult situation. You can ask for insight into an interpersonal relationship. You can ask just about anything you want and see what comes up. The more you work with runes, the stronger your ties to the symbols will become. You will begin to notice a pattern. The same symbols will come up for you and will get your attention.

Beyond asking questions, you can also tell the runes what you need. If you are ready to embark on a new endeavor or project, you could draw ⌐, *perth*, to channel the energy of Initiation. If you are traveling, you can call on the energy of Ψ, *algiz*, for Protection. If you feel anxious and need help calming your mind, you can pull |, *isaz*, the energy of Stillness. A favorite of mine that I see often in meditations is ᛞ, *dægaz*, which represents Breakthrough. When this rune appears to me, I am reassured that any form of struggle I may be experiencing at the moment, either in business or creatively, is leading me to a significant shift in thinking. I know that what may feel like a struggle now will lead to an outcome even better than what I've imagined.

I recently went into a meeting with a potential investor for the medical-grade meditation app that my team and I have been working on for the past eighteen months. We are gearing up for a medical trial in Athens, Greece, in partnership with a doctor who specializes in weight loss. I intentionally pulled ᚷ ᚧ ᚱ, which represent Fertility, Harvest, and Flow, so I could plant the seeds of those energies in this first meeting— which, fortunately, coincided with the new moon. I set the intention that this meeting would be the first of many and that we would arrive at an agreement that benefited both sides.

Interestingly, the meeting had initially been scheduled for the prior month but had been canceled fifteen minutes before it was supposed to start. Our lawyer met with us anyway to give us a pep talk so we didn't feel discouraged. I wasn't disappointed about the cancellation, as I have learned to say to myself, "Things are always working out for me!" I had faith that the meeting would happen and the new timing would be even better.

So when the meeting was rescheduled to take place on a new moon, I had validation. Armed with my three powerful runes—Fertility, Harvest, and Flow, carved in rose quartz—I went in with confidence. I was wearing a dress that had no pockets, so I tucked them safely in my bra, as the rune-savvy entrepreneur must occasionally do.

There are three easy ways to become more familiar with the runes:

* yes-or-no reading
* open-question one-rune daily pull
* three-rune situational pull

YES-OR-NO READING

The simplest way to begin working with the Runes is to ask a basic yes-or-no question and pull one stone. You can ask questions such as:

"Can I trust this person?"

"Is now a good time to change jobs?"

"Is this relationship the right one for me?"

"Am I seeing this situation clearly?"

The yes-or-no rune reading is helpful when you have a moment of doubt or indecision. Earlier this year, I was spending time with someone very close to me who was working through some personal issues. I had spent much of the day with him, but I was trying to balance supporting my friend with honoring my inner artist, who requires time alone at home. Despite my discomfort with doing so, I said goodbye to my friend and got in my car to drive home. I was two minutes down the road when I felt this very strong uncomfortable feeling in my gut. I wondered, "Ugh, what is *that?*" It was if something inside me answered, "Turn the car around." It was an overwhelming feeling that took me by surprise. For a moment, I felt strongly conflicted and couldn't decide what to do.

I pulled the car over and grabbed my bag of runes. I held the bag, closed my eyes, and asked aloud, "Is it in my best and highest interest to go back to be with my friend?" I pulled a rune and drew ᛉ, *algiz*, representing Protection. In this moment, I was not concerned with the specific rune I'd drawn; I just focused on the fact that I'd drawn the rune with the symbol facing me, which I took to be a *yes* answer to my question. I actually second-guessed the answer, which I never do, since in recent meditations I was being guided to spend more time alone versus with others. I modified my question and asked again, "So I should not go home right now?" I pulled another rune, and this time the symbol was facing away from me, meaning *no*, i.e., no, I should not go home. Tempting fate, I asked a third time. "Are you telling me I should turn this car around right now and go back to comfort my friend?" I pulled a third and final rune. This time it was ⌞, *perth*, which represents Initiation. The symbol facing me gave me a definitive answer: *Go back to be with your friend.*

"Okay, okay" I said. "I hear you."

Since I was pulled over on a dark rural road, I must have looked like I was in trouble. At that moment, a police car pulled up next to me. I rolled down my window, as did the officer.

"Everything okay?" asked the young cop.

"Yes," I answered. "I was undecided about where I needed to go, but I just got my answer."

"Okay, have a nice evening," he said as he drove away into the night.

Was it a coincidence that I pulled the rune symbol for Protection, and a police officer showed up? If so, coincidences like these happen all the time as you begin working with the runes more and more. Doing as I'd been guided to do, I returned to my friend's house. He looked relived and appreciative to see me. I settled in next to him on the couch and felt settled inside, knowing I was precisely where I needed to be at that moment. I was able to be completely present and at peace.

To become comfortable with this method, you can start with less significant questions before moving into major questions. Ready? Now it is your turn.

The steps are simple:

1. Hold your bag of runes in your hands. If you are using rune cards, shuffle them for several seconds or minutes as you quiet your mind.

2. Close your eyes. Relax by taking a few deep breaths in and out. Ask your yes-or-no question, either in your mind or out loud. The more specific you are, the better.

3. Without looking, pick one rune. If you are using stones, did you draw a rune with the symbol facing you, or facing away from you? If you are using cards, does the symbol appear right-side up or not?

4. If the symbol is facing you, consider this a *yes* answer to your question. If the symbol is not facing you, consider this a *no* answer.

5. Notice how you feel when you get your answer.

Do you feel relieved by your answer? I always do, and something inside of me always says, "That's exactly right," validating the answer. The few times the answer surprised me or shook me up in some way, it caused me to more deeply examine my feelings on the topic of interest. If I get a *no* to a question I thought I wanted a *yes* to, that tells me there is more to how I feel. I then sit with it, ponder, and walk away with a different level of self-awareness.

The yes-or-no method has never steered me wrong. The more you ask yes-or-no questions, the more confident you will become using the runes as your own personal GPS.

OPEN-QUESTION ONE-RUNE DAILY PULL

Have you ever woken up on the wrong side of the bed? The alarm goes off and you feel flooded by thoughts about your workday ahead, your lengthy to-do list, or all the undesirable things you need to get done? If the day begins with feelings of anxiety or dread, those feelings can cast a pall over the rest of the day. It is not unusual to let our humanness get the best of us.

Or perhaps the morning starts in a whirlwind. Everything feels like a mad dash: getting the kids ready, making the coffee, merging into rush-hour traffic, and on it goes.

The open-question one-rune pull is a way to hit the reset button to wash away any negative thoughts or to hit pause before facing the day, allowing us to center and focus. The runes can serve as a great tool for establishing a daily practice. When you pull one rune each morning and read its description, it will advise you on what you need to focus on for that day.

As you connect more and more with your runes, you may find over time that the symbols appear to you in your mind. If I close my eyes and tap in, I can ask a question and immediately see a rune symbol in my mind. In fact, I was seeing runes in my mind's eye way before I knew anything about them.

About four years ago, in the rare moments when my mind was quiet enough to notice, I would see a flash of a symbol that looked like this:

After several months of seeing this image, I finally asked my business partner Rita if she knew what it was. Rita is a gifted intuitive who specializes in spiritual therapy. We met in 2013 at a weekend-long mediumship workshop. At the time, I was climbing the corporate ladder, leading a research team at a Fortune 100 company in Connecticut. However, despite big bonuses and work I enjoyed, I felt like something was missing. I was unclear about my purpose and was just beginning a stage of soul searching.

I took a bold step and formed a limited liability company called Solstice Strategy Partners in July of that year, not knowing why it was to be named that. The word "solstice" came out of nowhere. When people would ask why, I would say, "I have no idea; I just know that's the name."

I also wasn't sure what the business would be about. I knew it would be consulting of some sort, yet I also sensed there would be another part of it that was still playing out.

I ended up meeting Rita two months later. Rita has been an intuitive her entire life, but at that time her gift was just starting to really blossom. It was in our very first exchange that she said to me, "We are going to be in business together." Without thinking, I replied, "I know." In the months that followed, Solstice Strategy Partners unfolded.

Now back to seeing ⚡. I asked Rita if she knew what that symbol was. She gazed off for just a moment as she tends to do when she is tapping in to the other side. Then she said, "Runes . . . you are to research and study the runes. I see you doing rune readings."

I asked, "What are runes?"

She said, "I have no idea. I've never heard the word until just now. You will remember them. You already know them."

Now, at the time, while I believed in her gift completely, I was not yet ready to own my own intuitiveness. I said, "Okay," but I was thinking, *There is no way I am doing rune readings anytime soon. That is way too far out there for me.* Talk about famous last words!

At some point after that conversation, I did a quick internet search on rune symbols and located the ⚡ rune that I kept seeing. Called *sowilo,* its literal translation is "sun," and it represents Wholeness. Well, that froze me in my tracks, because the image I used for the Solstice Strategy logo is a sun spray, which appears as follows:

I thought back to how compelled I was to name the business Solstice. It was too much of a coincidence to ignore.

For the next few years, Solstice evolved into a place of business where people came to heal and restore themselves to wholeness, which is ultimately the journey we are all on. Rita counseled hundreds of clients who were working through major life changes that ranged from divorce to career change, while I mentored business owners and their management teams to be more conscious and communicative leaders.

Interestingly, we never had a fear of failure (and still don't). We both left well-paying jobs to jump into the world of entrepreneurship with our eye on global change. The call to do this was so strong that nothing would stop us. In 2014 we boldly declared on our first website that we would affect one *billion* lives by 2020. While we had no idea how we would do that as two spiritual practitioners, we also knew that if we didn't put it out there, it would never happen.

Now called Cloud9 Online, Solstice has evolved into a health technology company with twenty amazing superhumans whom we refer to as our "soul family." We launched our first meditation app, called MediMind, in 2018 and have since been creating medical-grade meditation apps for hospitals to address chronic pain. Our charge is to tackle the opioid crisis head on by teaching people how they can self-heal both physical and emotional pain through meditation. With technology on our side, we know we can reach one billion lives! Although we just might need a *little* more time.

It would be several months after Rita shared her vision before I would embrace the runes, but the point is, the runes were speaking to me for years before I understood what they were. The runes played a central role in my intuitive development, which became more and more crucial as we further built out the business.

Cloud9 Online Creative Team, March 2018.
From left to right: Valerie Rogers, Sabrina John, Debra Lynn, Delanea Davis, Henry Edinger, Lynne Hartwell, John Odlum, Rita MacRae, Bradford Tilden

Starting today, create time to pull one rune to answer an open-ended question each day. Like brushing your teeth, make pulling this daily rune part of your normal routine. Consider what you want your open-ended question to be. Some typical examples are:

"What do I need to focus on today?"

"What should I be mindful of?"

You can be slightly more specific and ask things like:

"What insight do I need for my workday today?"

"What clarity do I need when it comes to my health?"

I personally prefer asking general questions like these when doing a one-rune pull. Take note if any particular rune feels familiar to you. Also notice what thoughts or feelings come up when you examine the rune you pull.

When you are ready, take the following steps:

1. Hold your bag of runes in your hands, or if you are using rune cards, shuffle them and pull a card you feel drawn to.

2. Close your eyes. Relax with a few deep breaths in and out. Ask either in your mind or out loud, "What do I need to be aware of today?" Then, draw one rune stone or card.

3. What rune did you pull? Draw it in the space below.

4. Look up the meaning of the rune symbol in part III. What
immediate association with the rune do you have, based on what
you read there and what is happening in your life right now?

_____

_____

_____

You may want to keep the rune in your pocket as a reminder of what
you need to focus on for the entire day. Or you can draw the rune symbol
in a place where you will see it throughout the day. I like to draw my
daily rune on the back of my hand, just below my left thumb.

I also recommend you journal about your experiences with the runes in
one of two ways. First, you can answer the pause-and-reflect questions that
accompany each rune in part III. You can answer these questions as you go,
after you pull that rune, or you can simply read the meaning of each rune
and answer the questions sequentially. Do what you feel most drawn to do.

Alternately, when you feel ready to begin you can start the thirty days
of journaling that part II of this book will guide you through. You will
begin with pulling a single rune as described above for seven days before
moving on to the three-stone situational rune pull for the next seven days.
Use the rune meanings in this book as a starting point, but also be open to
what thoughts, sensations, or emotions the rune triggers for you. Record
your observations.

You may notice that the same runes appear over and over again.
When this occurs, we should pay particular attention to the message.
For me, I take it to mean I am not fully internalizing that rune's meaning or heeding its advice. This is why certain runes will appear again and
again until the message is received.

In addition to reflecting or journaling, I recommend charting your
daily pulls for a full month so you can become more aware of the messages you're receiving. I tend to pull ᛗ, *mannaz,* frequently. *Mannaz* represents the Self, which is a reminder that everything emanates out from
us. The Law of Attraction is always in play. Whatever we put out with
our thoughts and actions comes back to us. When I hear my coaching

clients say, "I am so lucky to have such great people in my life," I remind them that it isn't luck. Like attracts like.

You draw in exactly what you put out. If you are what we call a positive, "high-vibration" person, you draw in other positive, high-vibration people. If you trend toward a lower vibration, you will attract less positive people. *Mannaz* reminds me that I am a powerful manifester. If I expect something to happen, it always does. For your dreams to become a reality, you must believe that dream or something better will inevitably come your way in due time. Identify the "what" of what you want, and leave the "how" up to the universe.

Record your daily pull in the journaling section so any patterns will stand out to you. I like to draw the rune symbol and write its alphabetic value and its one-word meaning like this:

SUNDAY	MONDAY	TUESDAY	WEDNESDAY	THURSDAY	FRIDAY	SATURDAY
Joy	Journey	Joy	Journey	Stillness	Movement	Protection
V	*R*	*V*	*R*	*I*	*E*	*Z*
ᛈ	ᚱ	ᛈ	ᚱ	ᛁ	ᛗ	ᛦ

THREE-RUNE SITUATIONAL PULL

Another way to work with the runes is to think about a specific area of your life where you feel you need guidance. For example, perhaps you want insight into a relationship with a friend, or you may be considering a career change. You would pull three runes and place them in a horizontal line from right to left as follows.

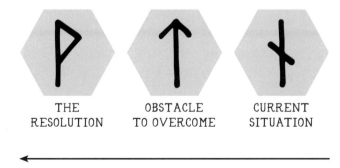

| THE RESOLUTION | OBSTACLE TO OVERCOME | CURRENT SITUATION |

The first rune, placed in the Current Situation position, will provide you with an overview of the situation you are asking about. It tells you what *is*.

The second rune, placed in the Obstacle to Overcome position, will highlight what you may need to consider to if you want the most favorable outcome possible. It tells you what you need to *do*.

The third rune, placed in the Resolution position, shows you what outcome is likely, especially if you heed the advice coming from the second-position rune. It tells you *what's possible*.

Note that in this spread you read the runes from right to left. This is the historical tradition, which I like to follow.

Below is a rune reading I recently did for a close friend while she was traveling over the holidays. She and her fiancé were taking her three small children on a five-hour train ride to visit her fiancé's family. I imagined her and asked for insight into the situation regarding her new blended family.

Again referencing Blum's work as my guide, here is what the runes revealed:

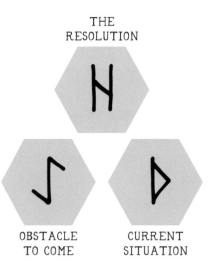

THE
RESOLUTION

OBSTACLE   CURRENT
TO COME   SITUATION

Current Situation: *Thurisaz,* or Gateway, invites you to understand your limitations and be aware that important decisions are at hand.

Pause and consider the big picture and what matters to you most before you act.

Obstacle to Overcome: *Eihwaz,* or Surrender, suggests the importance of doing the right thing to persevere. Maintain a flexible posture, and understand how much you have grown from past situations. Do not become frustrated by delays, should they arise. *Eihwaz* suggests both an end and a new beginning. Expect something or someone from the past to emerge so you can resolve it for good this time.

Resolution: *Hagalaz,* or Disruption, indicates there is an unexpected event coming; thus, it is best not to make any long-term plans at this time. This event will lead to significant change that will allow you to let go of the past, provide room for great growth, and give you a sense of freedom that you have not yet known.

When I shared this reading with her, her immediate association was with an imminent court date where she was finally facing her ex-husband regarding a child-custody agreement. The last five years had been very stressful for her and her children. After a series of life-changing events, my friend moved back to her hometown where she'd grown up. There she was able to draw upon the support of her parents and siblings and keep her children safe from their mentally unbalanced father.

Under normal circumstances it would be best for both parties to agree in advance to a joint-custody agreement, but she knew she would not be doing right by her children to allow their father to have joint decision-making authority when it came to their well-being. This meant she would walk into the trial and leave the fate of her children in the hands of the judge.

The rune reading spoke to the three-year delay as her ex kept blocking any sort of final legal agreement, which had caused her great frustration. She felt like the open-ended nature of things was preventing her from completely moving forward with her life. This much-anticipated court date marked the end of a chapter that she desperately wanted to close so she could fully enjoy what was coming next.

As this book was going to press, my friend's situation was still playing out, and we do not yet know what ᚺ, which represents Disruption, means for the Resolution. It indicates there will be an unexpected disruptive twist that is outside of her control. While it hints at causing some level of emotional pain, it will be cathartic and will allow her to finally release the past and embrace a better future.

Ready to give it a try for yourself? Follow these steps:

1. Hold your bag of runes in your hands, or shuffle your rune cards.

2. Close your eyes. Relax with a few deep breaths in and out, and think about an area in your life where you need insight or guidance. Ask either in your mind or out loud, "What do I need to know about this situation?" Then draw three runes and place them as depicted below.

3. Look up each meaning and take a moment to apply what you read to the situation you asked about. What insight did the Runes give you?

Record the Rune symbols in the spaces below:

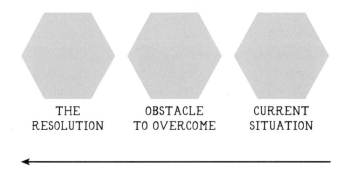

THE RESOLUTION   OBSTACLE TO OVERCOME   CURRENT SITUATION

PAUSE AND REFLECT

What situation in your life did you ask about?

_____

_____

_____

How does the Current Situation rune apply?

_____

_____

_____

Taking into account the rune for Obstacle to Overcome, what mind-set change or action is the rune encouraging you to undertake?

_____

_____

_____

What does the Resolution rune suggest to you?

_____

_____

_____

I always gain clarity and a fresh perspective when I use this three-rune pull. It's like giving your Higher Self a microphone and stage. Your Higher Self always has something meaningful to tell you when you prepare the stage.

SPECIFIC ASSISTANCE: POWER COMBINATIONS

Another way to use the runes is to combine them when you need extra support on any given day. Below are some rune combinations that resonate with me, although you are welcome to create your own power combinations.

POWER COMBINATIONS

Adventure	**Journey + Joy**
Ambition	Initiation + Flow
Balance	Growth + Gateway + Movement
Confidence	Warrior + Wholeness
Courage	Self + Strength + Protection
Creativity	Harvest + Flow
Direction	Signals + Opening
Faith	Protection + Journey
Focus	Breakthrough + Stillness
Freedom	Self + Inheritance + Initiation
Growth	Disruption + Breakthrough + Wholeness
Happiness	Flow + Joy + Wholeness
Independence	Inheritance + Fertility + Strength
Leadership	Constraint + Movement + Breakthrough
Mindfulness	Signals + Stillness
Passion	Opening + Partnership + Joy
Persistence	Fertility + Strength + Gateway
Pleasure	Self + Joy + Flow
Relaxation	Stillness + Wholeness
Security	Protection + Warrior + Gateway
Success	Abundance + Harvest + Wholeness
Trust	Self + Partnership + Unknown

If you want to invoke a certain emotional or mental state on any given day, you can select the corresponding combination of runes and keep them with you in your pocket for that day.

I am particularly fond of the power combination I created for *leadership:*

ᛏ Constraint—cautioning us to consider the outcome we want before we react instead of thoughtfully responding

ᛗ Movement—encouraging us to take a step forward for progress to occur

ᚺ Breakthrough—suggesting that the growing pains we feel always lead us to greater awareness and wisdom. The old adage "What doesn't kill us makes us stronger" is certainly true when we are in a leadership position, as well as in life in general.

Anytime something unexpected occurs in one of my companies, I generally do not get flustered. Instead I take it in neutrally and think, "Well, there is a first time for everything. What did I learn from this?" When the business loses out on a deal or encounters a delay, by now I know something even better, easier, and more fun is just around the corner.

When you begin to view life in this more even-handed way, everything flows with more ease. What you might have previously interpreted as bad or negative is perhaps instead the universe moving things around on your behalf to deliver an even more favorable outcome. With time, a little patience, and the runes, we can see this.

You can also experiment with creating a bindrune, which is a method for uniting two or more runes into a single runic symbol to supercharge them. Here are two examples.

Can you find at least five distinct runes in the first bindrune, and four in the second bindrune? What do you these combinations mean to you?

_____

_____

_____

_____

_____

_____

RUNES AND CELESTIAL BODIES

In a recent meditation, I explored a link between the runes, the celestial bodies in our solar system, and constellations. While the runes and astrology may seem like disparate systems, I strongly believe that all is connected. Everything—including people—is made of the same source energy. The runes, celestial bodies, and constellations are all viable systems for heightening the powers we hold within, and a connection across all systems exists if you want it to. It is all about the intentions you set.

Similar to Kabbalah meditation, where your mind is actively drawing Hebrew letters in various combinations as a form of prayer to manifest positive outcomes such as good health and angelic support, you can use the runes to tap into the power of the sun, the moon, and the planets of our solar system. The runes can form a portal that unlocks the energy of a celestial body and directs that energy back to our lives to give us more strength in an area where we need it most.

Given that I was born on a full moon in June of 1975, I have always been drawn to moon energy. I love to meditate and then journal during full moons, and whenever possible, I book meetings and life events in synchrony with moon cycles. New moons create the optimal energy for new beginnings for projects, business deals, and relationships of all forms. Full moons set the stage for completion of cycles and projects.

Waxing moons bring the energy of expansion and growth, while waning moons inspire releasing and reducing.

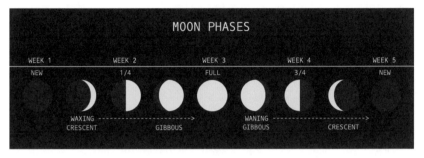

Cycles of the Moon

The following table illustrates which runes to use to attract the energies specific to the moon, the sun, and each planet.

CONNECTIONS BETWEEN RUNES AND CELESTIAL BODIES

CELESTIAL BODY	COSMIC ENERGY	CORRESPONDING RUNES
Sun	Self-expression, courage, self-confidence, risk taking, outward expression	⚡ Þ ᛗ
Moon	Emotions, intuition, security, receptivity	ᚠ ᛚ
Mercury	Intellect, reason, communication, language, curiosity	ᚱ ᛗ
Venus	Love, relationships, beauty, harmony, femininity	ᛩ ᛪ ᚷ
Mars	Action, aggression, competition, desire, passion, sex, masculinity	ᛏ ᛉ ᚲ
Jupiter	Expansion, growth, understanding, luck, success, optimism, knowledge	ᛒ ᚠ ᛪ
Saturn	Regulation, structure, responsibility, order, obligation, discipline	ᛁ ᛏ
Uranus	Unforeseen changes, rebellion, eccentricity, creativity, individuality	ᚺ ᚢ

CELESTIAL BODY	COSMIC ENERGY	CORRESPONDING RUNES
Neptune	Spirituality, subconscious, imagination, surrender, transcendence	ᛋ ᚲ
Pluto	Transformation, power, death and rebirth, evolution	ᚦ ᛗ

Now let's experiment with the amplified energy of the runes when coupled with cosmic energy by trying a visualization-based meditation. This meditation can be done with or without actual runes.

To begin, think about a situation or challenge in your life that requires more of you in some way. It might be the courage to take action (Mars), the confidence to be completely authentic (the sun), or the ability to open your heart more in a relationship (Venus). Once you select your situation and corresponding body, commit the corresponding rune symbols to memory. Then try the following meditation:

1. Find a comfortable place where you can relax and not be disturbed for at least ten minutes. Either sit or lie down with your legs and feet resting uncrossed. Close your eyes.

2. Take a deep breath in for a count of seven. Hold the breath for a count of four. Exhale fully for a count of eight. Repeat five times.

3. Visualize the night sky full of twinkling stars. Continue to breathe comfortably.

4. Visualize the celestial body of your choice. Now visualize each of the corresponding runes being drawn on the surface of that body in bright white light.

5. Once all the runes are drawn, hold them in your mind with your eyes still closed.

6. When you feel ready, imagine the bright light of each rune coming out of the sky all the way down to earth, entering the through the top of your head.

7. Feel the energy of the runes move slowly from the top of your head through your face, neck, chest, arms, torso, legs, and feet.

8. As you do this, feel your whole being connected to the sky as well as planted firmly on earth. Pay attention to how it feels when the runes and the celestial energy enter your body.

Journal your experience below. Capture as much detail as possible regarding what you saw and how you felt, both in your body and emotionally.

Celestial body focus in meditation: _____ Date: _____

Corresponding rune: _____

I chose this planet and corresponding runes because . . .

_____

_____

_____

_____

I saw . . .

_____

_____

_____

_____

I felt . . .

_____

_____

_____

_____

I am now more aware that . . .

_____

_____

_____

_____

RUNES FOR IMPROVING RELATIONSHIPS

In addition to obtaining clarity about yourself and situations in your life, you can also use runes to shed light on your relationships. When we are in something, we are often too close to it to evaluate where it's been, what it is today, what impedes it, and where it can go. We as humans often either romanticize things, focusing too much on what we hope it will be while overlooking the drawbacks, or we pay too much attention to what is wrong while taking for granted what is right.

Most of us will resort to asking a friend or family member for their perspective, but even our most well-intentioned friends have a perceptual filter through which they see the world. They will evaluate what we tell them based on their own life experiences and may project what's best for them onto us. Even when advice from friends and loved ones comes from a place of love and protection, it always carries an inherent bias.

The very best advice we can get regarding what is best for us comes from within, and asking about relationships is no different. The runes can open that channel for us. When searching for insight about capability, future potential, or conflict resolution, you can always use a yes-or-no pull, a one-rune pull, or a three-rune situational analysis. But if you want more depth, you can also use a five-rune pull in a layout known as the Runic Cross.

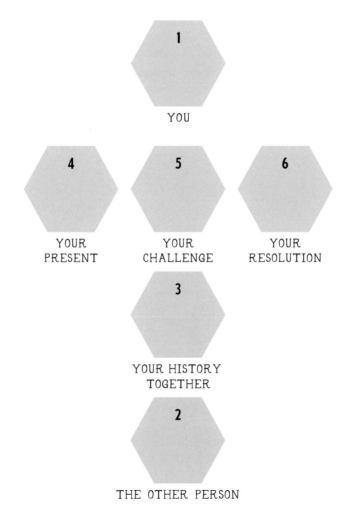

There are multiple ways to interpret the Runic Cross, but as with anything, the intention you set behind the reading informs what it means to you. That said, I read the Runic Cross as follows:

- Past
- Present
- Heart of the Matter
- Influencing Factors
- Challenge
- Resolution

If any area feels unclear, you can always pull an additional rune for more information if you feel drawn to do so.

RUNES FOR COUNSELING OTHERS

You can use the runes as a counseling tool to help a friend, a family member, or even a teenager who needs a new way of seeing things. This use of the runes is historically called a rune reading. Some may think that sounds like fortune-telling, but really a rune reading is a way for you to create a safe, sacred environment for someone to explore how they are feeling about things happening in their lives.

Just as for yourself, you can invite someone else to engage in the following rune exercises:

- yes-or-no reading
- one-rune pull
- three-rune pull
- Runic Cross

Instruct your counselee to close his or her eyes. Then ask them: "In a few sentences, in what area of your life do you require higher-level guidance?"

While they're holding the runes in their hands, tell them to take a moment to visualize the situation as if they are reliving it, bringing forth any natural emotions connecting them to the situation.

When they are ready, invite them to pull one, three, or five runes. I like to allow the other person to pull the stones themselves, but that is personal preference. If you feel you should be the only one to touch your runes, that is okay too.

As they pull each one, lay them out as previously instructed. First explain the layout, then explain what each rune means in relation to the position it occupies in the reading. When you are finished, allow the other person to respond.

To open up the conversation after reading the runes, you may ask, "Based on what I just said, what resonates?" or "How does this apply to what is happening in your life?"

Then sit back and listen while both sides of the person's mind—the rational and the creative—open up to a new way of seeing things. In nearly all situations, the person you read for will find some thread of meaning in what you say in your reading and will find a way to make it personally relevant. Try not to steer or lead your counselee in any way. This is their time to process, find meaning, and think about ideas inspired by the runes.

When I am reading for others, I like to use a blank sheet of paper to make notes about the rune spread. I write down the date, the name of each rune in the spread, and highlights of the reading so the person has a record of it. Often, so much information comes through in a rune reading that it becomes hard to take it all in. This is especially the case if the rune reading touches on emotional topics.

If you read for someone and they ask for additional information that was not covered in the rune reading, you can always pull additional runes to answer their questions.

NOTICING PATTERNS

The more you work with the runes, you will inevitably begin to notice patterns. You may find you pull the same one, two, or three runes repeatedly over the course of a week. This is an indication there is a strong message for you that you may be missing. If this occurs, challenge yourself by asking, "Why does this rune keep appearing? What am I to learn from this?"

One method for doing this is a practice I call the "five whys." This is a technique I use when I moderate focus groups or am coaching others to explore deeper feelings that go beyond surface-level rational thinking. Asking yourself "why" multiple times could lead you to a deeper meaning behind what you feel—and that meaning may surprise you.

Here is a personal example. I am very drawn to ᚹ, *wunjo*, which represents Joy. If I am making handmade rune jewelry, I always want to carve or paint this glyph. When I pull it as a daily or see it appear in a rune spread, I am always so happy and always say aloud, "I love *wunjo!*"

So . . . why? If you asked me that once, I would say, "I like to have fun. Anyone who knows me tends to say I have more fun in life than anyone they know." And this is true, but there is a lot more to it. So what do we learn if I ask myself five whys behind why I love pulling *wunjo?* Let's see:

Why? Because it makes me smile.

Why? Because the idea of joy reminds me of being a kid on Christmas.

Why? Because as an adult, I live in a world of pressure and responsibility, and I encounter a lot of unhappy people. These are all things I was unaware of as a child. Life then was very simple and full of leisure time and happiness.

Why? Because my dad and grandmother did a great job of shielding me from what was actually happening in the world just outside our home. I had no idea I had an institutionalized mother who was battling a bleak mental-health diagnosis and struggling with alcoholism.

Why? They did this for me out of love, and for that I am grateful.

Incredible, right? I am not one to dwell on the past, and I certainly do not spend time thinking about my mom occasionally being in a mental institution during my childhood. When I do think of my childhood, I recall climbing trees (I was a classic tomboy), making mix tapes by holding my tape recorder up to the TV on a Friday night, making blanket forts in the backyard, reading encyclopedias, and that epic Christmas Eve in 1983 when my godparents gave me a Cabbage Patch doll. I was so happy I cried! Those are the highlights of my childhood memories.

My narrative and playback of my childhood centers around creativity, nature, music, and unconditional love. While there was an undertone of missing my mom, I always had a feeling that anything was possible, and because I was never told anything different, I always believed just that: anything is possible. Most of my memories are joyful, and that is all thanks to my family, who loved me and protected me in my earliest, most vulnerable years.

So now it's your turn. Take a moment to look at all of the rune symbols. Decide which one are you most drawn to right now; it may be the rune you were drawn to earlier in this book, or it may be a different one. Then ask yourself the five whys, and write down your answers below.

I am most drawn to _____.

Why #1? _____

_____

Why #2? _____

_____

Why #3? _____

_____

Why #4? _____

_____

Why #5? _____

_____

RUNE CASTING

A more advanced way to work with the runes is called a rune cast. Rather than pulling a set number of runes, you hold all the runes in your hands, quiet your mind for a moment, and think about the area of your life in which you want guidance. I like to do this at the beginning of every new year. I hold the runes and ask, "What do I need to know about this upcoming year?"

You then allow the runes to fall out of your hands onto a table or cloth. If you like nature, you can allow the runes to fall on the sand of a beach or on the ground. You will notice that some runes fall with their symbols facing up, while others fall with their symbols face down. Start by removing all of the runes that are face down. When the face-up runes remain, you then use your intuition to segment them into clusters. Each cluster will be a "chapter." Your intuition will guide you regarding what each chapter will pertain to.

Each time I do a rune cast, my numbers of clusters and chapters vary. For example, this morning I did a rune cast for myself regarding motherhood, a topic that is very sensitive to me. As a highly career-focused woman of forty-three who miscarried four years ago, the teeter-totter between livelihood and motherhood is something I've struggled with for years. Do I pursue my dream of being a mom and risk it slowing me down in my calling to help people across the globe heal? Or do I let go of being a biological mother and continue on this wondrous journey of healing the self and teaching others to heal?

This is a common dilemma many of us face. Like everyone else, I feel the pressure of society and my biological clock saying, *Make a decision . . . you don't have a lot of time.* However, a voice as quiet as a whisper inside soothes me and says, *Stop worrying. Everything is going to be just fine.* In a situation as sensitive and momentous as this one, I consult the runes.

When I cast the runes in 2018 with motherhood in mind, here is what I got.

Intuitively, I sensed there were four clusters or chapters. The story begins in the upper left then proceeds clockwise as follows:

- Past: Surrender, Stillness, Breakthrough

- Present: Signals, Disruption, Joy, Wholeness

- Requirements: Partnership

- Final Outcome: Journey, Harvest

In the past sit Surrender, Stillness, and Breakthrough. How does that relate to my past, with regard to motherhood? The first few years of my marriage had high highs and low lows. I entered a blended family and became a stepmom of kids ages ten, fourteen, and sixteen. Having grown up in a harmonious household with a mom, dad, stepmom, and stepsister, I believed my new family would embrace me, and I saw myself having at least two children of my own. I had a hard time adjusting to being a stepparent, which delayed any efforts of trying to conceive. After four years and weighing all factors, I elected to undergo in vitro fertilization, believing it would be the fastest path to parenthood.

While successful at first, my pregnancy ended after eight weeks. My stepkids were unaware that I was ever pregnant to begin with, so keeping it a secret exacerbated the emotional pain of the loss. Until I went through it myself, I had no idea how many women have suffered the pain of miscarriage. It took years to heal from that experience.

Defensive (Surrender) and frozen (Stillness) was absolutely how I felt. The experience disconnected me from my husband. I felt this deep resentment that he'd already had the experience of bringing children into the world and felt their love each day, while I felt like an interloper, almost a stranger in my own home. Between the trials of their teenage years and my loss, I convinced myself that motherhood was not for me.

At that time that I quit my corporate job and started my first business, which became my figurative baby. Mistakenly, I thought this was my revelation (Breakthrough) when, in reality, the Breakthrough would not come for a few more years and would require a lot of courage and faith to leap into the great unknown to get to the clarity I so desperately needed.

In the present sit Signals, Disruption, Joy, and Wholeness. Today, I live in a little "creative house" twenty-five miles away from the house where I lived as a wife and stepmom. After eighteen months of living here with my rescue cats and dogs, I have been able to step into my creative flow, writing and leading two successful companies. My intuition (Signals) is at its highest peak. I am guided in everything I do as a result of my tie to the runes and the energetic channels they open for me.

It turned my life upside down (Disruption) to take steps to break away and live on my own, but through a series of runic consults and soul work, I knew I had to change my environment to learn about myself, shed my wounded skin, and grow. I could stay stuck in my own story of feeling like an invisible, unwanted stepmom who had lost a baby that no one could know about, or I could take a step to push forward. I knew I needed time and space to heal those wounds.

In time, the healing came. I became reacquainted with myself and discovered how much I liked being me. Hanging with me on a Friday night was a lot of fun. I established a practice of daily meditation and writing, starting as early as four a.m. on many days, and feel my soul sing (Joy) inside. It was from this quantum leap that the idea of this rune book came to be. Today I feel whole and complete (Wholeness) in a way I never have. In many ways I am happier than I have ever been.

The man who was my husband is no longer my wedded partner, but my connection with him is profoundly spiritual and deep. He co-owns and co-runs both of my companies with me. In addition, my relation-ship with his kids has blossomed into something I value and appreciate. They have grown into pretty incredible humans, and I love seeing them spread their wings and experience the world.

What's more, my connection with my guides has never been stron-ger. Most importantly, I love and respect myself completely. I am still a giving, loving, generous person, but I know I must take care of my needs first before I can take care of others. I sometimes wish I could go back to that tough time in my life with the tools I have now; it all could have been so much easier. But the soul's journey only knows one way—and that is from this moment forward.

So, with regard to motherhood, what is it I require? In a runic word, Partnership. I cannot do it alone. But I also cannot do it in a way that requires me to lose myself and my identity, as I have a habit of doing in romantic relationships. I can be a mother in a way that enhances my life, rather than bringing my life to a halt. It is not a binary deci-sion, even though many in society today suggest we as women have to choose between livelihood and motherhood. Not today; not anymore. Not for the kick-ass modern-day go-getters that we can now be. We get to have it all!

What's the final outcome to all of this? The runes are letting me know that, just like you, I am living and learning life lessons and on my own journey (Journey). I have been taking all the necessary steps and have done the hard work for the reward (Harvest) to come. While I may not be able to see the tangible fruit of my spiritual and emotional labor just yet, I am to trust that the bounty will be delivered.

Will this harvest result in an actual pregnancy and biological baby? I really don't know, but I am completely at peace with knowing that everything is as it should be and will unfold as it should. I feel complete trust. I know there is nothing to worry about, no sudden action I should take; I am to just allow it all to come to me however it is meant to come. In the state of Joy and Wholeness that I am perpetually in, everything feels divine.

RUNE CASTING FRAMEWORKS

I f casting runes on a blank slate and clustering them based on your intuition feels too abstract, you may prefer using some sort of framework. Sometimes when casting runes I imagine I am looking at a clock, and I see the chapters chronologically, as depicted below. I read the chapters beginning with the 7:00–10:00 section, which represents recurring lifelong themes. I then move to 10:00–12:00, which is a recap of the previous year. Then I move to 12:00–2:00, which is life right now, followed by six months from now, sitting at 2:00–5:00. I then finish at 5:00–7:00, which is one year from now. Should any runes land in the middle, I see this as life-lesson territory.

This framework provides a very straightforward way to practice, because it gives you two dimensions for applying the meaning of each rune and tying it to a certain time period in your life.

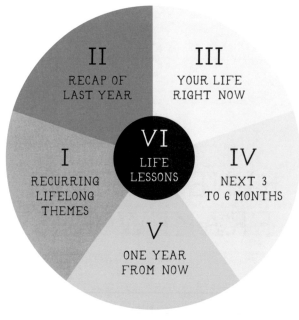

Chronological Wheel

Experiment and see what feels right to you. If you are using the cards at the back of this book, try turning them all face down in four rows and six columns. Hover your hand over each card, and flip the cards you feel drawn to. You may feel warmth or tingling over certain cards. Use your intuition, and have fun with it!

RUNE INNOVATIONS

Rune reading does not have to be limited to the ways of the Old Norse. Since I often use the runes as a teaching tool to make self-learning more fun, I like to experiment with new methods for reading the runes beyond the stones and wooden chips. Here are a few of my latest innovations.

"FREYA" INSPIRATION CARDS

I created a set of twenty-four inspiration cards to use as gifts for my friends and family. Each card summarizes a brief message associated with a rune. Rather than pulling runes, you can shuffle these hexagonal cards and pull one card for a daily inspiration. Each morning, I shuffle the cards and ask, "What message do I need today?" Then I pull a card and read it aloud, and I prop it on the mantel of my fireplace for a visual reminder of what I should focus on that day.

I've found that these cards appeal to people who don't yet have a daily practice and want a quick thirty-second method for doing something that touches self-care without the commitment of pulling stones or journaling.

RUNE CUBES

Here is a fun one! Being a tactile person who can't resist the local craft store on a rainy Sunday, I bought precut wooden cubes and a $15 wood-burning tool to create a set of four rune cubes, which are essentially runic dice.

The smell of burning wood takes me back to my grandfather's carpentry workshop when I was five years old. Did you know smell is the most powerful trigger of memory? I find the smell of burning wood and sawdust to be particularly grounding.

Since each wooden block has six sides, I felt drawn to represent Tyr, Heimdall, and Freya equally, twice per cube, as follows:

	TYR	HEIMDALL	FREYA
Cube 1	ᛏ ᛚ	ᚺ ᛇ	ᚠ ᚱ
Cube 2	ᛒ ᛝ	ᚾ ᛈ	ᚺ ᚲ
Cube 3	ᛖ ᛟ	ᛁ ᛉ	ᚦ ᚷ
Cube 4	ᛗ ᛞ	ᛃ ᛊ	ᚨ ᚹ

To use rune cubes, hold them in your hands and ask a question, such as, "What wisdom can be shed on this situation?" Here is an example of a question I just asked the cubes:

"What wisdom can be shared with regard to this book and my entire rune platform?"

Here was my toss:

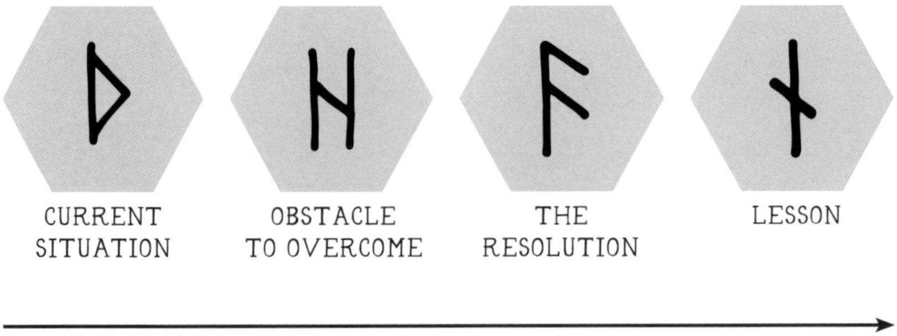
CURRENT SITUATION
OBSTACLE TO OVERCOME
THE RESOLUTION
LESSON

You may notice I chose to read them from left to right this time, as I was drawn to do so. Remember, the only real rules for the runes are the ones you create. Creating your own rituals is half the fun!

Here is what the runes are telling me: I am carrying some form of baggage that is slowing me down and making my path forward more arduous than it needs to be. I need to become aware of what I need to release to enable an easier way ahead. I hold on to this baggage or extra responsibility out of fear of the disruption it would cause to lighten my load. It is important to understand that the temporary disruption caused by letting go will allow something even better to grow in the newly created space.

When I can overcome this fear, there is an overflow of abundance in the form of love and freedom from all forms of constraint. The lesson I am to learn in all of this is to be clear about the outcome I want before reacting. In this case, if my ultimate goal is to hang out in my yurt and write more books with plenty of leisure time, then I must be willing to take a step back in one or both of the two companies I am running. That means bringing in a new leader to take my place and relinquishing most of the control I now have over both organizations.

My gut reaction: *scary!* But I know this is the message I need to hear. I know I am on the precipice of receiving everything I want; all I had to do was get clear and focused on what it is I want most, then get out of my own way (and head) to let it all come rushing in.

At times fear hinders us in our efforts to know and define exactly what we want. We may be afraid we'll never get it, or we may fear the changes in our lives caused by getting what we want. Also, we may crave so much certainty about the future that we become paralyzed with fear of the unknown. The more we can get comfortable with allowing life to unfold at a natural pace, the happier we become. There is no hiding from your truth when you bring the runes into the mix, as you will soon see.

PART II

THIRTY DAYS
OF PRACTICE

N ow let's embark on a thirty-day journey together to establish a daily practice of reading runes and get to know yourself better.

For the next thirty days, you will have a daily assignment that involves pulling one or more runes paired with a journaling practice. The thirty days are broken up into five flights.

DAYS 1–7: ESTABLISHING A DAILY PRACTICE

During your first week, you will establish a daily practice by pulling one rune each morning and then documenting its meaning and application in your life. You will also use the runes for yes/no questions, then journal your results.

DAYS 8–14: UNDERSTANDING SITUATIONS

During the second week, you will continue with your daily one-rune-pull practice. You will also do three-stone readings that analyze past and present situations in your life.

DAYS 15–21: KNOWING OTHERS

During the third week, you will continue with your daily one-rune-pull practice. You will also add in relationship readings to shed insight into key relationships in your life.

DAYS 22–28: MANIFESTING OUTCOMES

During the fourth week, as you continue with your daily one-rune-pull practice, you will select runes based on the energy you need to bring into your life each day, and you will journal the outcome.

DAYS 29–30: JOURNEY REFLECTION

In the final two days, you will consider what forms of rune readings resonated with you most. You will also be asked to review all your journal entries up to that point so you can consider what you have learned about yourself during your thirty-day journey. Be sure to give yourself at least two hours to review your entries and notice what came up for you over the course of the four weeks.

The ultimate goal of establishing a daily practice and journaling your experiences is to train your mind, body, and spirit to align. These exercises will strengthen your natural ability to know more about situations, others, and yourself. I call this ability *intuition,* but you can think about it any way you want.

When it comes to the journaling aspect of the practice, feel free to use the pause-and-reflect questions that correspond to each rune in part III of this book. These questions are meant to prompt you if you get stuck staring at a blank page. If you prefer open-form journaling without any prompts, then do that instead. Go by what feels right to you.

By the end of the thirty days, you will have developed a preference for how to work with the runes and when to read them. In the process, you will know how to directly connect with your Higher Self when you need guidance.

At some point in working with the runes, you may find that, like me, you do not need the actual stones or the modern-day meanings I have written. You may find that when you close your eyes, you start seeing rune symbols. For this reason, do your best to memorize the one-word meaning for each rune.

So if you ask, "What do I need to be aware of today?" and you see ᚱ, *raido,* which means Journey, you can then ask, "How is Journey significant for me today?" Then pay attention to the first thing that comes up for you. Your immediate impression is always right. If your first association is your career, then ask yourself, "How does Journey relate to my career"? Again, see what comes up. I like writing my intuitive impressions down because, just like dreams, these impressions are fleeting and easy to forget because they are not coming from our rational mind.

Don't fret if, after thirty days, you still need the runes and the modern meanings. Take it at your own pace. Use the runes and the meanings as long as you want to. Consider the runes and this book as training wheels that will teach you how to connect to your authentic self, all day, every day. Once this direct connection is achieved, it will be with you for the rest of your life.

Illustration by George Peters Designs

BEFORE YOU BEGIN

Before you start your thirty-day process, take a moment to answer these initial questions.

What do you hope to learn over the next thirty days?

_____

_____

_____

_____

What drew you to using the runes as a self-discovery tool?

_____

_____

_____

_____

_____

_____

_____

_____

Are you willing to devote fifteen to thirty minutes each day to fully experience the runes? At what time of day? Where?

_____

_____

_____

_____

_____

_____

_____

_____

_____

THIRTY-DAY SUMMARY

As you move through the next thirty days, document which rune you pull for your daily one-rune reading in the grid below. Record the runic symbol, the one-word description, and the corresponding alphabetic letter, and notice whether any symbols repeat.

SUNDAY	MONDAY	TUESDAY	WEDNESDAY	THURSDAY	FRIDAY	SATURDAY

Which rune symbols repeated over the course of the month?

_____

_____

_____

_____

How do those runes hold particular significance for you?

_____

_____

_____

_____

Were any words spelled out to you?

_____

_____

_____

_____

What else do you notice?

_____

_____

_____

_____

DAYS 1–7: ESTABLISHING A DAILY PRACTICE

DAY 1: DAILY FOCUS

Ask yourself "What do I need to focus on today?" and then pull a rune.

Symbol: _____ One-word meaning: _____ Letter: _____

How does this rune apply to what is happening in your life today?

_____

_____

_____

_____

_____

_____

_____

_____

_____

_____

_____

_____

_____

_____

_____

_____

_____

_____

_____

_____

DAY 1: YES/NO

What yes/no question do you have for today?

_____

_____

_____

_____

Pull a rune and record whether you received a yes (symbol face up) or no (symbol face down).

❏ **YES**   ❏ **NO**

Why is this question important to you?

_____

_____

_____

_____

VALIDATION

What happened? Was the rune guidance accurate or helpful?

_____

_____

_____

_____

DAY 2: DAILY FOCUS

Ask yourself "What do I need to focus on today?" and then pull a rune.

Symbol: _____ One-word meaning: _____ Letter: _____

How does this rune apply to what is happening in your life today?

_____

_____

_____

_____

_____

_____

_____

_____

_____

_____

_____

_____

_____

_____

_____

_____

_____

_____

_____

_____

_____

DAY 2: YES/NO

What yes/no question do you have for today?

_____

_____

_____

_____

Pull a rune and record whether you received a yes (symbol face up) or no (symbol face down).

❏ **YES**   ❏ **NO**

Why is this question important to you?

_____

_____

_____

_____

VALIDATION

What happened? Was the rune guidance accurate or helpful?

_____

_____

_____

_____

DAY 3: DAILY FOCUS

Ask yourself "What do I need to focus on today?" and then pull a rune.

Symbol: _____ One-word meaning: _____ Letter: _____

How does this rune apply to what is happening in your life today?

_____

_____

_____

_____

_____

_____

_____

_____

_____

_____

_____

_____

_____

_____

_____

_____

_____

_____

_____

_____

_____

_____

DAY 3: YES/NO

What yes/no question do you have for today?

_____

_____

_____

_____

Pull a rune and record whether you received a yes (symbol face up) or no (symbol face down).

❏ **YES**　　　　❏ **NO**

Why is this question important to you?

_____

_____

_____

_____

VALIDATION

What happened? Was the rune guidance accurate or helpful?

_____

_____

_____

_____

DAY 4: DAILY FOCUS

Ask yourself "What do I need to focus on today?" and then pull a rune.

Symbol: _____ One-word meaning: _____ Letter: _____

How does this rune apply to what is happening in your life today?

_____

_____

_____

_____

_____

_____

_____

_____

_____

_____

_____

_____

_____

_____

_____

_____

_____

_____

DAY 4: YES/NO

What yes/no question do you have for today?

_____

_____

_____

_____

Pull a rune and record whether you received a yes (symbol face up) or no (symbol face down).

❏ **YES**   ❏ **NO**

Why is this question important to you?

_____

_____

_____

_____

VALIDATION

What happened? Was the rune guidance accurate or helpful?

_____

_____

_____

_____

DAY 5: DAILY FOCUS

Ask yourself "What do I need to focus on today?" and then pull a rune.

Symbol: _____ One-word meaning: _____ Letter: _____

How does this rune apply to what is happening in your life today?

_____

_____

_____

_____

_____

_____

_____

_____

_____

_____

_____

_____

_____

_____

_____

_____

_____

_____

_____

_____

DAY 5: YES/NO

What yes/no question do you have for today?

_____

_____

_____

_____

Pull a rune and record whether you received a yes (symbol face up) or no (symbol face down).

❏ **YES**   ❏ **NO**

Why is this question important to you?

_____

_____

_____

_____

VALIDATION

What happened? Was the rune guidance accurate or helpful?

_____

_____

_____

_____

DAY 6: DAILY FOCUS

Ask yourself "What do I need to focus on today?" and then pull a rune.

Symbol: _____ One-word meaning: _____ Letter: _____

How does this rune apply to what is happening in your life today?

_____

_____

_____

_____

_____

_____

_____

_____

_____

_____

_____

_____

_____

_____

_____

_____

_____

_____

_____

DAY 6: YES/NO

What yes/no question do you have for today?

_____

_____

_____

_____

Pull a rune and record whether you received a yes (symbol face up) or no (symbol face down).

❏ **YES**   ❏ **NO**

Why is this question important to you?

_____

_____

_____

_____

VALIDATION

What happened? Was the rune guidance accurate or helpful?

_____

_____

_____

_____

DAY 7: DAILY FOCUS

Ask yourself "What do I need to focus on today?" and then pull a rune.

Symbol: _____ One-word meaning: _____ Letter: _____

How does this rune apply to what is happening in your life today?

_____

_____

_____

_____

_____

_____

_____

_____

_____

_____

_____

_____

_____

_____

_____

_____

_____

_____

_____

_____

_____

DAY 7: YES/NO

What yes/no question do you have for today?

_____

_____

_____

_____

Pull a rune and record whether you received a yes (symbol face up) or no (symbol face down).

❏ **YES** ❏ **NO**

Why is this question important to you?

_____

_____

_____

_____

VALIDATION

What happened? Was the rune guidance accurate or helpful?

_____

_____

_____

_____

DAYS 8–14:
UNDERSTANDING
SITUATIONS

DAY 8: DAILY FOCUS

Ask yourself "What do I need to focus on today?" and then pull a rune.

Symbol: _____ One-word meaning: _____ Letter: _____

How does this rune apply to what is happening in your life today?

_____

_____

_____

_____

_____

_____

_____

_____

_____

_____

_____

_____

_____

_____

_____

_____

_____

_____

_____

DAY 8: UNDERSTANDING SITUATIONS

Think about a current situation in your life that requires clarity.

The situation is:

_____

_____

_____

_____

Consider this situation as you hold your runes. Then pull three runes and record each symbol from right to left. Be sure to write the one-word meaning for each rune in the boxes below as well.

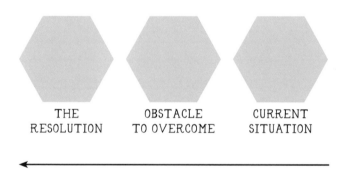

| THE RESOLUTION | OBSTACLE TO OVERCOME | CURRENT SITUATION |

What insight is shed on the situation based on your rune pull?

_____

_____

_____

_____

DAY 9: DAILY FOCUS

Ask yourself "What do I need to focus on today?" and then pull a rune.

Symbol: _____ One-word meaning: _____ Letter: _____

How does this rune apply to what is happening in your life today?

_____

_____

_____

_____

_____

_____

_____

_____

_____

_____

_____

_____

_____

_____

_____

_____

_____

_____

_____

DAY 9: UNDERSTANDING SITUATIONS

Think about another situation in your life that requires clarity.

The situation is:

_____

_____

_____

_____

Consider this situation as you hold your runes. Then pull three runes and record each symbol from right to left. Be sure to write the one-word meaning for each rune in the boxes below as well.

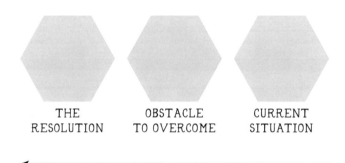

| THE | OBSTACLE | CURRENT |
| RESOLUTION | TO OVERCOME | SITUATION |

←—————————————————————————

What insight is shed on the situation based on your rune pull?

_____

_____

_____

_____

DAY 10: DAILY FOCUS

Ask yourself "What do I need to focus on today?" and then pull a rune.

Symbol: _____ One-word meaning: _____ Letter: _____

How does this rune apply to what is happening in your life today?

_____

_____

_____

_____

_____

_____

_____

_____

_____

_____

_____

_____

_____

_____

_____

_____

_____

_____

DAY 10: UNDERSTANDING SITUATIONS

Think about a current situation in your life that requires clarity.

The situation is:

_____

_____

_____

_____

Consider this situation as you hold your runes. Then pull three runes and record each symbol from right to left. Be sure to write the one-word meaning for each rune in the boxes below as well.

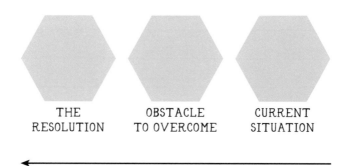

THE   OBSTACLE   CURRENT
RESOLUTION   TO OVERCOME   SITUATION

What insight is shed on the situation based on your rune pull?

_____

_____

_____

_____

DAY 11: DAILY FOCUS

Ask yourself "What do I need to focus on today?" and then pull a rune.

Symbol: _____ One-word meaning: _____ Letter: _____

How does this rune apply to what is happening in your life today?

_____

_____

_____

_____

_____

_____

_____

_____

_____

_____

_____

_____

_____

_____

_____

_____

_____

DAY 11: UNDERSTANDING SITUATIONS

Think about a current situation in your life that requires clarity.

The situation is:

_____

_____

_____

_____

Consider this situation as you hold your runes. Then pull three runes and record each symbol from right to left. Be sure to write the one-word meaning for each rune in the boxes below as well.

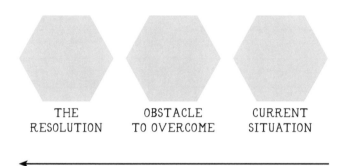

THE
RESOLUTION

OBSTACLE
TO OVERCOME

CURRENT
SITUATION

What insight is shed on the situation based on your rune pull?

_____

_____

_____

_____

DAY 12: DAILY FOCUS

Ask yourself "What do I need to focus on today?" and then pull a rune.

Symbol: _____ One-word meaning: _____ Letter: _____

How does this rune apply to what is happening in your life today?

_____

_____

_____

_____

_____

_____

_____

_____

_____

_____

_____

_____

_____

_____

_____

_____

_____

_____

_____

_____

DAY 12: UNDERSTANDING SITUATIONS

Think about a past situation in your life that requires clarity.

The situation is:

_____

_____

_____

_____

Consider this situation as you hold your runes. Then pull three runes and record each symbol from right to left. Be sure to write the one-word meaning for each rune in the boxes below as well.

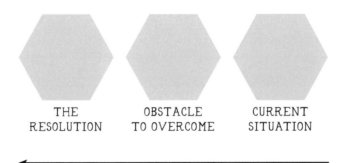

THE	OBSTACLE	CURRENT
RESOLUTION	TO OVERCOME	SITUATION

⟵──────────────────────────────

What insight is shed on the situation based on your rune pull?

_____

_____

_____

_____

DAY 13: DAILY FOCUS

Ask yourself "What do I need to focus on today?" and then pull a rune.

Symbol: _____ One-word meaning: _____ Letter: _____

How does this rune apply to what is happening in your life today?

_____

_____

_____

_____

_____

_____

_____

_____

_____

_____

_____

_____

_____

_____

_____

_____

_____

_____

DAY 13: UNDERSTANDING SITUATIONS

Think about another past situation in your life that requires clarity.

The situation is:

_____

_____

_____

_____

Consider this situation as you hold your runes. Then pull three runes and record each symbol from right to left. Be sure to write the one-word meaning for each rune in the boxes below as well.

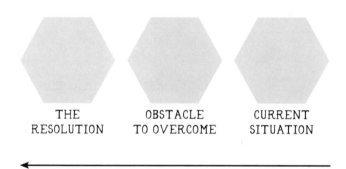

| THE RESOLUTION | OBSTACLE TO OVERCOME | CURRENT SITUATION |

What insight is shed on the situation based on your rune pull?

_____

_____

_____

_____

DAY 14: DAILY FOCUS

Ask yourself "What do I need to focus on today?" and then pull a rune.

Symbol: _____ One-word meaning: _____ Letter: _____

How does this rune apply to what is happening in your life today?

_____

_____

_____

_____

_____

_____

_____

_____

_____

_____

_____

_____

_____

_____

_____

_____

_____

_____

_____

_____

_____

DAY 14: UNDERSTANDING SITUATIONS

Think about another situation in your life that requires clarity.

The situation is:

_____

_____

_____

_____

Consider this situation as you hold your runes. Then pull three runes and record each symbol from right to left. Be sure to write the one-word meaning for each rune in the boxes below as well.

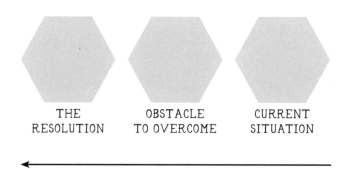

| THE RESOLUTION | OBSTACLE TO OVERCOME | CURRENT SITUATION |

What insight is shed on the situation based on your rune pull?

_____

_____

_____

_____

11

DAYS 15–21:
KNOWING OTHERS

DAY 15: DAILY FOCUS

Ask yourself "What do I need to focus on today?" then pull a rune.

Symbol: _____ One-word meaning: _____ Letter: _____

How does this rune apply to what is happening in your life today?

_____

_____

_____

_____

_____

_____

_____

_____

_____

_____

_____

_____

_____

_____

_____

_____

_____

_____

_____

_____

DAY 15: KNOWING OTHERS

Think of a person in your life who is significant to you today or has been significant in your past.

Record their name:

_____

_____

_____

_____

Hold your bag of runes and visualize this person standing face to face with you. Ask for insight regarding why this person has been a significant part of your life. Then pull six runes and record them sequentially in the space below.

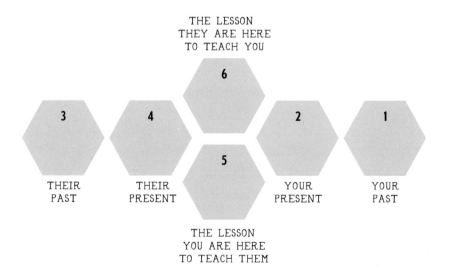

THE LESSON
THEY ARE HERE
TO TEACH YOU

6

3   4   2   1

5

THEIR   THEIR   YOUR   YOUR
PAST   PRESENT   PRESENT   PAST

THE LESSON
YOU ARE HERE
TO TEACH THEM

What is your first impression of this runic spread? How does it make you feel?

_____

_____

_____

What do the runes tell you about yourself?

_____

_____

_____

What do the runes tell you about them?

_____

_____

_____

What lesson are you here to teach this person?

_____

_____

_____

What lesson is this person here to teach you?

_____

_____

_____

What other thoughts and feelings do you have?

_____

_____

_____

DAY 16: DAILY FOCUS

Ask yourself "What do I need to focus on today?" and then pull a rune.

Symbol: _____ One-word meaning: _____ Letter: _____

How does this rune apply to what is happening in your life today?

_____

_____

_____

_____

_____

_____

_____

_____

_____

_____

_____

_____

_____

_____

_____

_____

_____

_____

_____

_____

_____

DAY 16: KNOWING OTHERS

Think of a person in your life who is significant to you today or has been significant in your past.

Record their name:

_____

_____

_____

_____

Hold your bag of runes and visualize this person standing face to face with you. Ask for insight regarding why this person has been a significant part of your life. Then pull six runes and record them sequentially in the space below.

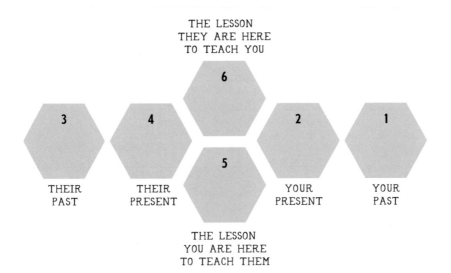

What is your first impression of this runic spread? How does it make you feel?

_____

_____

_____

What do the runes tell you about yourself?

_____

_____

_____

What do the runes tell you about them?

_____

_____

_____

What lesson are you here to teach this person?

_____

_____

_____

What lesson is this person here to teach you?

_____

_____

_____

What other thoughts and feelings do you have?

_____

_____

_____

DAY 17: DAILY FOCUS

Ask yourself "What do I need to focus on today?" and then pull a rune.

Symbol: _____ One-word meaning: _____ Letter: _____

How does this rune apply to what is happening in your life today?

_____

_____

_____

_____

_____

_____

_____

_____

_____

_____

_____

_____

_____

_____

_____

_____

_____

_____

_____

_____

_____

DAY 17: KNOWING OTHERS

Think of a person in your life who is significant to you today or has been significant in your past.

Record their name:

_____

_____

_____

_____

Hold your bag of runes and visualize this person standing face to face with you. Ask for insight regarding why this person has been a significant part of your life. Then pull six runes and record them sequentially in the space below.

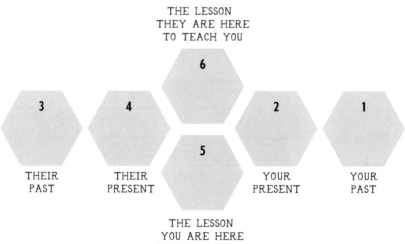

What is your first impression of this runic spread? How does it make you feel?

_____

_____

_____

What do the runes tell you about yourself?

_____

_____

_____

What do the runes tell you about them?

_____

_____

_____

What lesson are you here to teach this person?

_____

_____

_____

What lesson is this person here to teach you?

_____

_____

_____

What other thoughts and feelings do you have?

_____

_____

_____

DAY 18: DAILY FOCUS

Ask yourself "What do I need to focus on today?" and then pull a rune.

Symbol: _____ One-word meaning: _____ Letter: _____

How does this rune apply to what is happening in your life today?

_____

_____

_____

_____

_____

_____

_____

_____

_____

_____

_____

_____

_____

_____

_____

_____

_____

_____

_____

DAY 18: KNOWING OTHERS

Think of a person in your life who is significant to you today or has been significant in your past.

Record their name:

_____

_____

_____

_____

Hold your bag of runes and visualize this person standing face to face with you. Ask for insight regarding why this person has been a significant part of your life. Then pull six runes and record them sequentially in the space below.

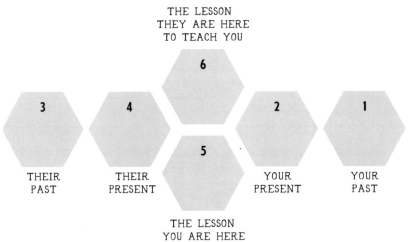

THE LESSON
THEY ARE HERE
TO TEACH YOU

6

3   4   2   1

5

THEIR   THEIR   YOUR   YOUR
PAST   PRESENT   PRESENT   PAST

THE LESSON
YOU ARE HERE
TO TEACH THEM

What is your first impression of this runic spread? How does it make you feel?

_____

_____

_____

What do the runes tell you about yourself?

_____

_____

_____

What do the runes tell you about them?

_____

_____

_____

What lesson are you here to teach this person?

_____

_____

_____

What lesson is this person here to teach you?

_____

_____

_____

What other thoughts and feelings do you have?

_____

_____

_____

DAY 19: DAILY FOCUS

Ask yourself "What do I need to focus on today?" and then pull a rune.

Symbol: _____ One-word meaning: _____ Letter: _____

How does this rune apply to what is happening in your life today?

_____

_____

_____

_____

_____

_____

_____

_____

_____

_____

_____

_____

_____

_____

_____

_____

_____

_____

_____

_____

DAY 19: KNOWING OTHERS

Think of a person in your life who is significant to you today or has been significant in your past.

Record their name:

_____

_____

_____

_____

Hold your bag of runes and visualize this person standing face to face with you. Ask for insight regarding why this person has been a significant part of your life. Then pull six runes and record them sequentially in the space below.

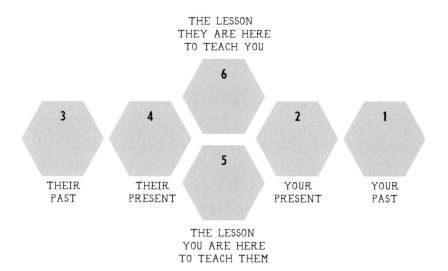

What is your first impression of this runic spread? How does it make you feel?

_____

_____

_____

What do the runes tell you about yourself?

_____

_____

_____

What do the runes tell you about them?

_____

_____

_____

What lesson are you here to teach this person?

_____

_____

_____

What lesson is this person here to teach you?

_____

_____

_____

What other thoughts and feelings do you have?

_____

_____

_____

DAY 20: DAILY FOCUS

Ask yourself "What do I need to focus on today?" and then pull a rune.

Symbol: _____ One-word meaning: _____ Letter: _____

How does this rune apply to what is happening in your life today?

_____

_____

_____

_____

_____

_____

_____

_____

_____

_____

_____

_____

_____

_____

_____

_____

_____

_____

_____

DAY 20: KNOWING OTHERS

Think of a person in your life who is significant to you today or has been significant in your past.

Record their name:

_____

_____

_____

_____

Hold your bag of runes and visualize this person standing face to face with you. Ask for insight regarding why this person has been a significant part of your life. Then pull six runes and record them sequentially in the space below.

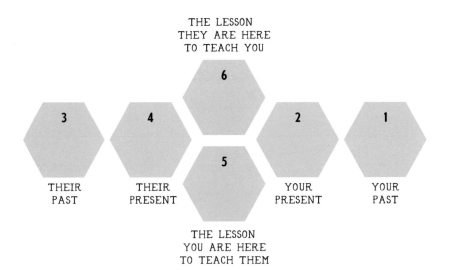

What is your first impression of this runic spread? How does it make you feel?

_____

_____

_____

What do the runes tell you about yourself?

_____

_____

_____

What do the runes tell you about them?

_____

_____

_____

What lesson are you here to teach this person?

_____

_____

_____

What lesson is this person here to teach you?

_____

_____

_____

What other thoughts and feelings do you have?

_____

_____

_____

DAY 21: DAILY FOCUS

Ask yourself "What do I need to focus on today?" and then pull a rune.

Symbol: _____ One-word meaning: _____ Letter: _____

How does this rune apply to what is happening in your life today?

_____

_____

_____

_____

_____

_____

_____

_____

_____

_____

_____

_____

_____

_____

_____

_____

_____

_____

_____

_____

_____

DAY 21: KNOWING OTHERS

Think of a person in your life who is significant to you today or has been significant in your past.

Record their name:

_____

_____

_____

_____

Hold your bag of runes and visualize this person standing face to face with you. Ask for insight regarding why this person has been a significant part of your life. Then pull six runes and record them sequentially in the space below.

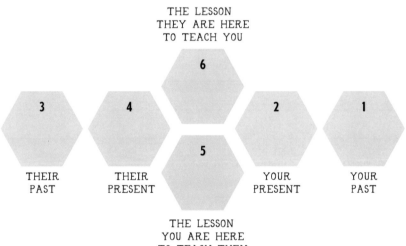

What is your first impression of this runic spread? How does it make you feel?

_____

_____

_____

What do the runes tell you about yourself?

_____

_____

_____

What do the runes tell you about them?

_____

_____

_____

What lesson are you here to teach this person?

_____

_____

_____

What lesson is this person here to teach you?

_____

_____

_____

What other thoughts and feelings do you have?

_____

_____

_____

DAYS 22–28:
MANIFESTING
OUTCOMES

DAY 22: DAILY FOCUS

Ask yourself "What do I need to focus on today?" and then pull a rune.

Symbol: _____ One-word meaning: _____ Letter: _____

How does this rune apply to what is happening in your life today?

_____

_____

_____

_____

_____

_____

_____

_____

_____

_____

_____

_____

_____

_____

_____

_____

_____

_____

_____

DAY 22: MANIFESTING OUTCOMES

What is happening in your day today?

_____

_____

_____

_____

What outcomes would you like to manifest?

_____

_____

_____

_____

Given this, from which of the twenty-four runic energies or combinations of energies would you benefit most today?

_____

_____

_____

_____

Now pull the runes you chose above. While holding them in your hands, state the following mantra to activate them:

> *I call on the energy of [state Germanic rune names] today to assist me with [describe situation]. By calling on this energy, I have all the support, protection, and confidence I need to manifest the best outcome.*

Then either keep the stones with you all day today, or simply draw the rune symbol or combination of symbols where you can see it throughout the day.

DAY 23: DAILY FOCUS

Ask yourself "What do I need to focus on today?" and then pull a rune.

Symbol: _____ One-word meaning: _____ Letter: _____

How does this rune apply to what is happening in your life today?

_____

_____

_____

_____

_____

_____

_____

_____

_____

_____

_____

_____

_____

_____

_____

_____

_____

_____

_____

DAY 23: MANIFESTING OUTCOMES

What is happening in your day today?

_____

_____

_____

_____

What outcomes would you like to manifest?

_____

_____

_____

_____

Given this, from which of the twenty-four runic energies or combinations of energies would you benefit most today?

_____

_____

_____

_____

Now pull the runes you chose above. While holding them in your hands, state the following mantra to activate them:

> *I call on the energy of [state Germanic rune names] today to assist me with [describe situation]. By calling on this energy, I have all the support, protection, and confidence I need to manifest the best outcome.*

Then either keep the stones with you all day today, or simply draw the rune symbol or combination of symbols where you can see it throughout the day.

DAY 24: DAILY FOCUS

Ask yourself "What do I need to focus on today?" and then pull a rune.

Symbol: _____ One-word meaning: _____ Letter: _____

How does this rune apply to what is happening in your life today?

_____

_____

_____

_____

_____

_____

_____

_____

_____

_____

_____

_____

_____

_____

_____

_____

_____

_____

_____

DAY 24: MANIFESTING OUTCOMES

What is happening in your day today?

_____

_____

_____

_____

What outcomes would you like to manifest?

_____

_____

_____

_____

Given this, from which of the twenty-four runic energies or combinations of energies would you benefit most today?

_____

_____

_____

_____

Now pull the runes you chose above. While holding them in your hands, state the following mantra to activate them:

> *I call on the energy of [state Germanic rune names] today to assist me with [describe situation]. By calling on this energy, I have all the support, protection, and confidence I need to manifest the best outcome.*

Then either keep the stones with you all day today, or simply draw the rune symbol or combination of symbols where you can see it throughout the day.

DAY 25: DAILY FOCUS

Ask yourself "What do I need to focus on today?" and then pull a rune.

Symbol: _____ One-word meaning: _____ Letter: _____

How does this rune apply to what is happening in your life today?

_____

_____

_____

_____

_____

_____

_____

_____

_____

_____

_____

_____

_____

_____

_____

_____

_____

_____

_____

_____

DAY 25: MANIFESTING OUTCOMES

What is happening in your day today?

_____

_____

_____

_____

What outcomes would you like to manifest?

_____

_____

_____

_____

Given this, from which of the twenty-four runic energies or combinations of energies would you benefit most today?

_____

_____

_____

_____

Now pull the runes you chose above. While holding them in your hands, state the following mantra to activate them:

> *I call on the energy of [state Germanic rune names] today to assist me with [describe situation]. By calling on this energy, I have all the support, protection, and confidence I need to manifest the best outcome.*

Then either keep the stones with you all day today, or simply draw the rune symbol or combination of symbols where you can see it throughout the day.

DAY 26: DAILY FOCUS

Ask yourself "What do I need to focus on today?" and then pull a rune.

Symbol: _____ One-word meaning: _____ Letter: _____

How does this rune apply to what is happening in your life today?

_____

_____

_____

_____

_____

_____

_____

_____

_____

_____

_____

_____

_____

_____

_____

_____

_____

_____

_____

_____

_____

DAY 26: MANIFESTING OUTCOMES

What is happening in your day today?

_____

_____

_____

_____

What outcomes would you like to manifest?

_____

_____

_____

_____

Given this, from which of the twenty-four runic energies or combinations of energies would you benefit most today?

_____

_____

_____

_____

Now pull the runes you chose above. While holding them in your hands, state the following mantra to activate them:

> *I call on the energy of [state Germanic rune names] today to assist me with [describe situation]. By calling on this energy, I have all the support, protection, and confidence I need to manifest the best outcome.*

Then either keep the stones with you all day today, or simply draw the rune symbol or combination of symbols where you can see it throughout the day.

DAY 27: DAILY FOCUS

Ask yourself "What do I need to focus on today?" and then pull a rune.

Symbol: _____ One-word meaning: _____ Letter: _____

How does this rune apply to what is happening in your life today?

_____

_____

_____

_____

_____

_____

_____

_____

_____

_____

_____

_____

_____

_____

_____

_____

_____

_____

_____

DAY 27: MANIFESTING OUTCOMES

What is happening in your day today?

_____

_____

_____

_____

What outcomes would you like to manifest?

_____

_____

_____

_____

Given this, from which of the twenty-four runic energies or combinations of energies would you benefit most today?

_____

_____

_____

_____

Now pull the runes you chose above. While holding them in your hands, state the following mantra to activate them:

> *I call on the energy of [state Germanic rune names] today to assist me with [describe situation]. By calling on this energy, I have all the support, protection, and confidence I need to manifest the best outcome.*

Then either keep the stones with you all day today, or simply draw the rune symbol or combination of symbols where you can see it throughout the day.

DAY 28: DAILY FOCUS

Ask yourself "What do I need to focus on today?" and then pull a rune.

Symbol: _____ One-word meaning: _____ Letter: _____

How does this rune apply to what is happening in your life today?

_____

_____

_____

_____

_____

_____

_____

_____

_____

_____

_____

_____

_____

_____

_____

_____

_____

_____

_____

_____

_____

_____

DAY 28: MANIFESTING OUTCOMES

What is happening in your day today?

_____

_____

_____

_____

What outcomes would you like to manifest?

_____

_____

_____

_____

Given this, from which of the twenty-four runic energies or combinations of energies would you benefit most today?

_____

_____

_____

_____

Now pull the runes you chose above. While holding them in your hands, state the following mantra to activate them:

> *I call on the energy of [state Germanic rune names] today to assist me with [describe situation]. By calling on this energy, I have all the support, protection, and confidence I need to manifest the best outcome.*

Then either keep the stones with you all day today, or simply draw the rune symbol or combination of symbols where you can see it throughout the day.

DAYS 29–30:
JOURNEY REFLECTION

DAY 29: DAILY FOCUS

Ask yourself "What do I need to focus on today?" and then pull a rune.

Symbol: _____ One-word meaning: _____ Letter: _____

How does this rune apply to what is happening in your life today?

_____

_____

_____

_____

_____

_____

_____

_____

_____

_____

_____

_____

_____

_____

_____

_____

_____

_____

_____

DAY 29: REVIEWING YOUR PROGRESS

Now that you are immersed in using the runes to better understand yourself, situations, and important relationships, take a moment to consider which forms of readings appeal most to you.

You have learned and practiced the following forms of readings:

- one-stone daily pull
- yes/no reading
- three-stone situational reading
- five-stone relationship reading
- manifesting outcomes with the runes

Which reading format resonates most with you?

\
\
\
\

Why?

\
\
\
\

Which reading format resonates with you the least?

\
\
\
\

Why?

_____

_____

_____

_____

Have you experimented with or used the runes in any other way?

_____

_____

_____

_____

Have you seen rune symbols while meditating or dreaming?

_____

_____

_____

_____

What patterns have you noticed? Have specific runes appeared over and over again when you pull runes?

_____

_____

_____

_____

If so, what do the patterns suggest to you?

_____

_____

_____

_____

DAY 30: DAILY FOCUS

Ask yourself "What do I need to focus on today?" and then pull a rune.

Symbol: _____ One-word meaning: _____ Letter: _____

How does this rune apply to what is happening in your life today?

_____

_____

_____

DAY 30: DISCOVERY REVIEW

As you finish your last day, please take a moment to read all of your entries over the past thirty days.

List three things you have learned about yourself.

1._____

_____

_____

_____

2._____

_____

_____

_____

3._____

_____

_____

_____

Based on what you've learned, what is one thing you are willing to start doing to be truer to yourself?

_____

_____

_____

_____

What is something you know you must continue doing to maintain your own personal happiness?

_____

_____

_____

_____

What is something you are willing to stop doing so you can move forward in your life?

_____

_____

_____

_____

How do you see your life right now?

_____

_____

_____

_____

PART III

MODERN MEANINGS OF THE RUNES

SYMBOL	PROTO-GERMANIC NAME	ONE-WORD MEANING	CORRESPONDING LETTER	PAGE NO.
ᚠ	Ansuz	Signals	A	182
ᛒ	Berknan	Growth	B	184
ᚲ	Kanu	Opening	C, K, Q	186
ᛗ	Dægaz	Breakthrough	D	188
ᛖ	Ehwaz	Movement	E	190
ᚠ	Fehu	Abundance	F	192
ᚷ	Gebo	Partnership	G	194
ᚺ	Hagalaz	Disruption	H	196
ᛁ	Isaz	Stillness	I	198
ᛃ	Jera	Harvest	J	200
ᛚ	Laguz	Flow	L	202
ᛗ	Mannaz	The Self	M	204
ᚾ	Naudiz	Constraint	N	206
ᛟ	Opila	Inheritance	O	208
ᛈ	Perth	Initiation	P	210
ᚱ	Raido	Journey	R	212
ᛊ	Sowilo	Wholeness	S	214
ᛏ	Teiwaz	Warrior	T	216
ᚢ	Uruz	Strength	U	218
ᚹ	Wunjo	Joy	V, W	220
ᚦ	Thurisaz	Gateway	TH	222
ᛇ	Eihwaz	Surrender	Y	224
ᛉ	Algiz	Protection	Z	226
ᛜ	Ingwaz	Fertility	NG	228
Blank	None	The Unknown	None	230

n the following pages I present an overview of the runes: their names, meanings, associations, and uses.

For each rune I give its proto-Germanic name. As mentioned earlier, some runes have more than one name; for simplicity's sake, I provide the proto-Germanic name I feel most drawn to.

I also provide a basic pronunciation for each rune name. Scholars of Old and Middle English may debate various pronunciations, but again, I offer this information for practical use rather than academic purposes.

In addition, I list a one-word meaning for each rune. Many other books on runes offer more complicated explanations of each rune, dissecting the meanings contained in the anonymously written Poetic Edda and in poems written by Icelandic author Snorri Sturluson in the 1200s. Scholars may say that is the proper way to interpret the runes; however, my goal is not to analyze history but rather to provide you with an interpretation that is relatable and relevant today, without relying unduly on writings that may be incomplete. As the old saying goes, history is written by the winners. We don't know what we don't know. Everyone has their own filters when interpreting and retelling history. All that said, I am very comfortable with bringing forward what each rune is telling us *today*, leaving the academic interpretations to the academics.

Finally, to offer a deeper understanding of each modern meaning, I share each rune's cosmic tie to astrological planets and signs. Runic purists may not agree with the blending of two seemingly disparate systems, but I find that this cosmic parallel gives each rune more dimension.

If you are struggling to apply the modern meaning of a rune to your life, this section provides pause-and-reflect questions that can prompt you to apply the meaning to the situations you are inquiring about. If you find these prompts useful, feel free to journal them if you are drawn to do so.

ANSUZ

ᚠ

Letter: A
Pronunciation: AWN-sooz
One-word meaning: Signals
Cosmic tie: ☾♋

....

Ansuz connects to the **moon**, which has the power to evoke our instincts, unconscious mind, and nurturing impulses. As such, this rune is associated with **Cancer**, the most emotional sign of the zodiac.

Modern meaning: Our intuition speaks to us in many ways: through dreams, hunches, fleeting thoughts, creative bursts, and even other people. On a daily basis, we are surrounded by signals and signs that we can easily miss if we are not aware of all the elements around us.

This rune invites you to connect to your own intuitive channel so you can navigate through life with more ease. Become more aware when thoughts, ideas, or inspirations come to you seemingly out of the blue. Similar to a GPS, this is what it feels like to tap into our very own divine guidance system. Our Higher Self is constantly sending us messages, pointing us to the path of least resistance.

The more open you are to these intuitive messages that are transmitted to you, the more messages you will receive. Spend ten minutes alone in a quiet place today. Take three deep breaths with your eyes closed, and practice asking for messages from your Higher Self. Ask, "What do I need to know today?" or "How can I solve this conflict?"

Ask any question, and the answer will be given in some form. Be open to how your question is answered. Trust the first answer you get to be the right one, as it is coming from the very best source: inside of you.

PAUSE AND REFLECT

What is the last fleeting thought you had that popped into your head out of the blue?

Close your eyes and ask yourself, "What does that mean?"

Do you trust your gut? Why or why not?

WRAP UP

We all possess innate intuitive abilities. When *ansuz* appears, we are being encouraged to pay attention to the signals and signs happening all around us and to recognize that they are often messages coming to us from a place of divine wisdom.

BERKNAN

ᛒ

Letter: B
Pronunciation: BEAR-kana
One-word meaning: Growth
Cosmic tie: ♃ ♐

....

Berknan connects to **Jupiter,** which conjures the energy of luck, success, optimism, expansion, and learning. This rune is associated with **Sagittarius,** the luckiest sign of the zodiac.

Modern meaning: As we move through life, birth, growth, and death are inevitable. However, the pace at which we grow—mentally, physically, emotionally, and spiritually—can vary from person to person. Sometimes we underestimate our own growth and overestimate the growth of others.

When we underestimate our own growth, we may be unnecessarily hard on ourselves and miss how much we've overcome; this is, after all, the process from which we learn. We don't give ourselves credit for the miles we've traveled to get to where we are today.

When we overestimate the growth of others, we may feel disappointed that they did not meet our expectations. In both cases, we are placing judgment on ourselves and others. Perhaps we're missing that we are *all* on a journey and we *all* grow with experience. We cannot force growth on ourselves or others.

We must understand and accept where we are, each on a unique journey, rather than placing expectations on what should be.

PAUSE AND REFLECT

Over the last five years, in which areas of your life have you grown the most?

What experiences led to that growth?

Call to mind a person in your life who disappointed or disappoints you. Can you reframe that disappointment in your mind and understand that the person is doing the best they can?

WRAP UP

Sometimes our most significant growth comes from painful experiences. When *berknan* appears, we are being reminded that we are here to learn and grow. We can embrace all experiences, even difficult ones, and see them as a challenge that will help us move on to the next level of learning.

KANU

Letter: C, K, Q
Pronunciation: KA-new
One-word meaning: Opening
Cosmic tie: ♆ ♓

Kanu draws from the energy of **Neptune**, the planet associated with idealism, spirituality, surrender, and transcendence. This rune connects strongly to **Pisces**, the wisest and most loving of the zodiac signs.

Modern meaning: A door is about to open before you, and with it, new possibilities. It is an opportunity you may miss if you are not aware and listening. Often, when there is a forward motion we want, we fixate on how we think it needs to unfold. When we do this, we may unintentionally block alternate paths to the outcome we desire.

For example, if you are unhappy in a current relationship, you may believe you will only be happy and feel fulfilled if you end it completely. The underlying need may be that you want to feel respected by the people in your life. Once you understand this, you may discover that it is time to speak up and establish boundaries with others rather than walk away from those who unknowingly cross a line with you.

Be mindful of what you want to change in your life, and explore why. Be open to how the universe can provide what you ask. In doing this, you allow multiple openings to deliver what you want. Be open. Be mindful. Be present. A new beginning awaits you in a form you may not have yet considered.

PAUSE AND REFLECT

How do you feel when new opportunities present themselves to you?

What one thing do you wish would change in your life?

What three possible forms might that change take?

WRAP UP

When *kanu* appears, we are encouraged to keep our minds open to an unexpected invitation or something we may not have previously considered. When we are approachable and open to new possibilities, sometimes magic can unfold.

DÆGAZ

Letter: D
Pronunciation: DAH-gaz
One-word meaning: Breakthrough
Cosmic tie: ♇♏

....

Dægaz is strongly connected to **Pluto**, the planet associated with power, transformation, and rebirth. Its astrological counterpart is **Scorpio**, the most intense and sexual of the zodiac signs.

Modern meaning: After trial and error, and after a series of stops and starts, you are on the brink of complete clarity—and with it, something significant. It may come in the form of a personal or professional achievement, or it may be the start of a new and better you.

It may be a creative breakthrough, something you have worked hard for in your career or at school, or a monumental change in a close personal relationship. While the path to what you want may have been long and bumpy thus far, the struggle you have been experiencing will be well worth it. Continue to push forward in moments of self-doubt and fear. Know that the universe is always working for your highest and greatest benefit. Be clear about what you want to happen, and trust that it will come to you.

It is time to take a deep breath, relax, and allow. The resolution you have been longing for is just a few steps ahead. Trust the process, and know you are exactly where you are meant to be in this moment.

PAUSE AND REFLECT

What is the one thing you have been struggling with or stuck on the most?

In this scenario, what is the worst thing that could happen?

Might there be another outcome you haven't considered? What could it be?

WRAP UP

The release and resolution you have been craving are right around the corner. *Dægaz* reminds you that when you stop trying to catch the butterfly, it may land right on your nose. Sit back and allow that breakthrough to come to you.

EHWAZ

M

Letter: E
Pronunciation: EH-waz
One-word meaning: Movement
Cosmic tie: ☿ ♊

....

Ehwaz is associated with the planet **Mercury**, the planet that fuels travel, communication, and thought. This rune is connected to **Gemini**, the zodiac sign known as "the twins" for its duality in nature.

Modern meaning: If you've been feeling stalled or stagnant in some area of your life—such as a relationship, your career, or perhaps your health—the time has come for a significant shift.

Now is a time for progress and forward motion. This may require physical movement, such as a trip or a physical change of address to get the proverbial ball in motion. The universe wants to support you now more than ever. However, you must have faith that a better life awaits, and be ready to take a first step to set the proverbial wheels in motion.

Begin with stating an affirmation that you are ready for change. Be specific about the area of your life in which this change must take place. Then, take a step. Even a small step will do. Momentum must begin with you. Then the true movement you are asking for will come.

PAUSE AND REFLECT

In what areas do you feel stagnant?

If you had a magic wand and could change this area of your life for the better, how would you change it?

What small step can you take today toward this outcome?

WRAP UP

Ehwaz invites us to embrace movement and motion in our lives. We are reminded that we have the power to manifest the life we truly want. Let go of what is, and open to what could be.

FEHU

ᚠ

Letter: F
Pronunciation: FEH-who
One-word meaning: Abundance
Cosmic tie: ♃ ♐

....

Fehu connects to **Jupiter**, which conjures the energy of luck, success, optimism, expansion, and learning. This rune is associated with **Sagittarius**, the luckiest sign of the zodiac.

Modern meaning: Often we feel safe because of the things we have, the people around us, or the place where we live. Our feeling of well-being comes from our possessions and a societal definition of what it means to be "rich." Many people emphasize external forms of wealth rather than an internal feeling of wealth.

However, the external forms of wealth—such as the car we drive, the jewelry we wear, or the home in which we live—can be fleeting. The things we have today can be gone tomorrow. We may "have it all" but still feel unfulfilled inside.

The time has come to explore what is inside you, to recast your view of what wealth and possessions are in order to truly reflect the genuine wealth of what is within you. Perhaps you are a nurturer, a protector, an artist, or a role model to others. Who you are inside can never be lost or taken away. Look within and take inventory of the gifts with which you came into this world. Become aware of all the natural talents you possess. Your life is full of abundance. As you shift your interpretation of wealth to focus on all that makes you special and unique, the more fulfilled and joyful your life will become.

PAUSE AND REFLECT

What does "wealth" mean to you? Do you feel wealthy now? Why or why not?

What natural talents do you possess?

What natural talent makes you feel most special?

WRAP UP

When *fehu* appears, we are reminded that wealth can be measured in many ways and that intangible wealth has the ability to fulfill us in a way that merely gathering more things cannot. Contemplate what is truly valuable.

GEBO

X

Letter: G
Pronunciation: GEH-boe
One-word meaning: Partnership
Cosmic tie: ♀♎♉

....

Gebo ties to **Venus**, the planet known for its feminine energy, inspiring romance, love, and beauty. As such, this rune is connected with **Libra**, the most balanced of all the signs of the zodiac, and **Taurus**, the most stable of the signs.

Modern meaning: A new union is coming your way that will require cooperation on your part to achieve the joy you are seeking at this stage of your life. While you can achieve much of what you desire on your own, it is time to allow someone inside the walls you have built around your heart. Although this may feel uncomfortable at first, it is okay to be vulnerable. You are not meant to be on this leg of your journey alone. This union may take the form of a new close friend, a new partner in a business endeavor, or a romantic partner. Whatever form this union takes, be open to it.

This union will have an energy of its own, different from any other relationship in your past. Resist comparing it or judging it against previous experiences. With your growth has come expansion. No longer do relationships define who you are. They are instead an enhancement to your life.

Allow your light to shine brightly from the inside out. Notice who you attract into your life, and allow new bonds to form. You are ready for this.

PAUSE AND REFLECT

What does partnership mean to you?

In what ways can a partnership with someone enhance your life?

When you think about partnering or joining forces with someone else to achieve a goal, how does it make you feel?

WRAP UP

Gebo invites us to let go of the limiting belief that we have to always do everything on our own. It's okay to ask for help when we need it and to accept that help when it is offered.

HAGALAZ

H

Letter: H
Pronunciation: HA-ga-las
One-word meaning: Disruption
Cosmic tie: ᚺ ♒

Hagalaz is strongly tied to **Uranus,** the planet that evokes sudden change, creativity, individuality, and eccentricity. This rune is connected with **Aquarius,** the most conscious and humanitarian sign of the zodiac.

Modern meaning: When we miss the subtle hints that it is time for us to make a change in our lives, sometimes the universe creates this change on our behalf so we can move to our next phase of learning.

A disruptive force is headed your way, but have no fear. This imminent change is coming because of a subconscious desire you have for a better life, even if you didn't yet formulate what you want or how you want it. You may have been suppressing this desire for fear of how it would play out. Let this worry go. The ending of a chapter marks the start of a new one, and with it comes light, hope, and infinite possibilities.

You are supported and loved in ways beyond what you can see, touch, and know. Trust that when this tidal wave of disruption unfolds, it will be for your highest and greatest good. You will come out on the other end happier and more whole. Change is inevitable. Embrace it with an open heart, and know that the outcome will be beautiful.

PAUSE AND REFLECT

What is the most challenging thing that has happened in your life so far?

What did that experience teach you?

In times of trouble, what are three things you can do to stabilize during sudden changes?

WRAP UP

Hagalaz inspires us to have faith in what we cannot yet see and trust that what waits for us on the other side of this mysterious transformation will be best for all parties involved.

ISAZ

|

Letter: I
Pronunciation: EE-saw
One-word meaning: Stillness
Cosmic tie: ♄ ♑

....

Isaz is strongly tied to **Saturn**, the planet associated with restraint, time, lessons, and responsibility. This rune is tied to **Capricorn**, the most steady and persistent of all the zodiac signs.

Modern meaning: Stillness is required at this time. Release any feelings of impatience or frustration with the lack of motion you may be experiencing. Our tendency as humans is to go-go-go, when sometimes what we really need is to unplug and just be still. Physical and emotional rest is also what your soul needs to recharge and refresh.

When something in our lives comes to an unexpected or abrupt halt, our faith in the universe and in ourselves can be challenged. When we are in the midst of it, it is easy to fall into a victim mentality. We may say, "Why is this happening to me? What did I do to deserve this?" However, over time we may come to realize that the halt was for the best.

It is important to remind ourselves that in any given moment, we do not always have all the information or wisdom explaining why something has come to a standstill. The key is to believe it is what we need and therefore must be for a better tomorrow. Embrace this pause and rest.

PAUSE AND REFLECT

What is the first word or image you see when you say the word "stillness" aloud?

Is your association with stillness positive or negative? Why?

What is the biggest barrier in your life within your control that prevents you from inviting more stillness into your life?

WRAP UP

When *isaz* appears, we are reminded that all things are in divine order all the time—even when it feels like we've hit a wall. Allow yourself to be in quietude today, and enjoy the much-needed rest and rejuvenation it brings.

JERA

Letter: J
Pronunciation: YAR-ah
One-word meaning: Harvest
Cosmic tie: ♀♎♉

Jera ties to **Venus**, the planet known for its feminine energy, inspiring romance, love, and beauty. As such, this rune is connected with **Libra**, the most balanced of all the signs of the zodiac, and **Taurus**, the most stable of the signs.

Modern meaning: Harvest is an understanding of what we have and the infinite potential we possess as human and spiritual beings. Harvest connects us to the bounty and beauty in life: our surroundings, our home, our relationships. Harvest is a reminder to take stock of all we have and make time each day for reflection. It also allows for a jumping-off point to see what is possible and to understand that more bounty is available to us.

Gratitude is the key to receiving more: more love, more positive experiences, more joy. Absolutely anything is possible if we take the time to appreciate what we have, share what we have, and find several reasons each day to say thank you.

Enjoy the fruits of your labor and all your hard work. You deserve all that you have, and there is more to come as you continue to appreciate the bounty.

PAUSE AND REFLECT

Name three things for which you are grateful.

What forms of bounty do you have in your life that you may take for granted?

What is an example of something you crave but perhaps don't need?

WRAP UP

When *jera* appears, we are invited to pause and reflect on all we have and release any craving we may carry for what we do not have. The hard work is done. Enjoy the bounty that already surrounds you.

LAGUZ

ᛚ

Letter: L
Pronunciation: LA-gooz
One-word meaning: Flow
Cosmic tie: ☾♋

....

Laguz connects to the **moon,** which has the power to evoke our instincts, unconscious mind, and nurturing impulses. As such, this rune is associated with **Cancer,** the most emotional sign of the zodiac.

Modern meaning: The time has come for you to hit your stride. Now is when all things will come to you and move through you with ease and grace. Creative bursts, answers to questions, and solutions to problems all unfold before you effortlessly. Obstacles melt away. Challenges resolve. Conflicts dissipate. Be particularly aware of your thoughts and language throughout the day. Your words, your mindset, and your actions must all be framed with the outcomes you desire. Believe anything is possible, and so it will be.

When we achieve this natural state of flow, all things move and groove. We lose track of time and are joyfully immersed in what we are doing. For some, flow enables immense creativity. For others, flow triggers complete focus. For all of us, flow activates creation. It allows us to manifest the things we want when we want them.

If tapping into this flow zone is a challenge for you today, change your scenery. Take a day trip somewhere you've never been. Seek out beautiful things such as art, music, or nature. These things can inspire flow. Activate your flow today, and see what new ideas or expressions arise.

PAUSE AND REFLECT

When in your life do you experience flow naturally?

What does flow feel like to you?

In what circumstances do you need flow most in your life?

WRAP UP

When *laguz* appears, we are reminded that while creativity and clarity can flow through us spontaneously, we can also ask for our days to unfold with ease, joy, and grace. Set this simple intention, and enjoy the ride.

MANNAZ

ᛗ

Letter: M
Pronunciation: MAH-naz
One-word meaning: The Self
Cosmic tie: ☉♌

....

Mannaz connects to the **sun**, which rules vitality and individuality. As such, this rune is associated with **Leo**, the most loyal sign of the zodiac.

Modern meaning: Life can be complicated and overwhelming at times. You move so fast and are responsible for so much. You put the needs of others before your own so often that you are missing *you* deep down. You may perceive doing something nice for yourself as unnecessary. This is not the case. You matter. You deserve to treat yourself as well as you treat others. When this happens, it is an opportunity to take time to recenter and breathe.

Become aware of what you want and need in life, starting with today. In those fleeting quiet moments when you are alone, really ask yourself what happiness means to you. You need to answer this for yourself before you can express it to others and take action.

This knowing comes from within the Self, inside of you. Give yourself permission to put yourself first today. It all starts with knowing what you want, having the courage to say it out loud, then going for it. You deserve it. It's time to give back some of that glorious love to yourself.

PAUSE AND REFLECT

What does happiness mean to you?

What is within your control versus what is beyond your control?

If you had a magic wand and could make any change to be happier, what would you change?

WRAP UP

When *mannaz* appears, we are gently reminded to make time for self-care so we can rest and recharge. Get a massage, go for a walk in the woods, or eat a pink cupcake! Do something special today to honor and celebrate you.

NAUDIZ

Letter: N
Pronunciation: NOW-deez
One-word meaning: Constraint
Cosmic tie: ♄ ♑

Naudiz is strongly tied to **Saturn**, the planet associated with restraint, time, lessons, and responsibility. This rune is tied to **Capricorn**, the most steady and persistent of all zodiac signs.

Modern meaning: Sometimes in sensitive or unexpected situations we may react and say things we do not mean without considering the ultimate impact our words may have on others. We may be too emotional in a rational situation, or too rational in an emotional one. It is important for us to recognize that words have power. This rune invites us to take a necessary pause to reflect about the outcome we want before we respond in a heated moment.

When faced with a challenging situation involving another person, consider using a pausing phrase, such as, "I need some time to think about that." This allows you to step away from the situation, take a deep breath, and consider what you want to happen next. Then you can craft your response accordingly. You possess the ability to inspire harmony rather than discord if you allow yourself a moment of stillness and clarity before engaging.

PAUSE AND REFLECT

What is an example of a situation where you reacted in haste and then regretted what you said or did? How would you respond now?

What are your trigger situations or people that set you to react instead of thoughtfully responding?

What pause phrase will you use to give yourself time to step away from a situation before you react?

WRAP UP

When *naudiz* appears, we are being asked to pause and put ourselves in the other person's shoes. Consider where they are before communicating in a way that may be hurtful or counterproductive. Choose your words with grace and compassion today.

OPILA

Letter: O
Pronunciation: OH-pila
One-word meaning: Inheritance
Cosmic tie: ♃ ♐

....

Opila connects to **Jupiter**, which conjures the energy of luck, success, optimism, expansion, and learning. This rune is associated with **Sagittarius**, the luckiest sign of the zodiac.

Modern meaning: Who we are and how we express ourselves comes from our ancestral roots. How far back we choose to look can have an extreme impact on our appearance, mindset, and emotional disposition today.

At times of self-doubt or insecurity, we may recall past experiences that we interpret as explaining our current flaws or inadequacies. We may assign blame to what we perceive as a physical limitation, such as our weight, our financial constraints, or an emotional block we may have due to an adverse circumstance.

If we allow ourselves to look back much further, to ancient times of pharaohs, seers, and priestesses, we can connect with the most honorable and prestigious parts of our birthright. At a DNA level, we are all of these things. We each possess a unique tie to the divine. We all possess infinite beauty and knowledge. Our capacity to love and be love transcends time.

Consider what you wish you could be when you envision the ultimate you, knowing that you already are that and more.

PAUSE AND REFLECT

When you think of the word "inheritance," what is the first person, place, or thing that comes to mind?

What have you consciously inherited from your family lineage?

What famous person in history have you always felt drawn to? Why? What in that person do you see in yourself today, even if only slightly?

WRAP UP

When *opila* appears, we are being reminded to hold our heads high and be proud of all parts of ourselves. Step into all that makes you spectacular. What is yours is yours and has always been. Celebrate beautiful you.

PERTH

Letter: P
Pronunciation: pearth
One-word meaning: Initiation
Cosmic tie: ☿♈

....

Perth is strongly tied to **Mars,** the planet that sparks drive, aggression, and masculine energy. Its corresponding sign is **Aries,** the most spontaneous and restless sign of the zodiac.

Modern meaning: It is time to take the first step toward the change you have been contemplating. Passively waiting for something to move you down this path is not creating the change you seek. Taking an active and assertive disposition is what the universe requires to deliver to you what you want. It is okay not to have a fully baked plan or know exactly how it will all unfold. You don't have to know all the details, but you do have to do something. Even the smallest step will inspire motion.

If you have avoided taking a step forward out of self-doubt or fear, the time has come to release it. If a financial limitation has delayed you, know that there is more than one way to obtain what you want. If you are worried that this change you desire may hurt others, you are being encouraged to think about yourself at this juncture of your life. There is no such thing as the "right time" or "wrong time" for changes. Everything is divinely timed and unfolds as it is supposed to.

No more thinking. It is time for doing. You are supported and loved. Decide you are ready, then take the leap.

PAUSE AND REFLECT

What are the things you know you want to change right now?

Is there something within your control that you want to change?

What one step can you take today to start down the path toward this change?

WRAP UP

When *perth* appears, we are being pushed to take decisive action. First we must be clear in our hearts and minds about the change we want. Then we must take that first courageous step forward. Take that leap, and trust that the universe will do the rest.

RAIDO

R

Letter: R
Pronunciation: RA-dough
One-word meaning: Journey
Cosmic tie: ☿♊

....

Raido is associated with the planet **Mercury**, the planet that fuels travel, communication, and thought. This rune is connected to **Gemini**, the zodiac sign known as "the twins" for its duality in nature.

Modern meaning: Each morning when we wake, we can take steps forward in our journey, or we can stand in place. We can choose the illuminated path of living, laughing, loving, and learning; or we can choose the shadowed path where we stand still and focus on everything that is wrong. When we chose the path of light, we are growing and expanding, which is what we each came here to do. When we choose a path of dimness or darkness, we are denying our soul the ability to grow.

Regardless of which path we take, we are each on our own unique journey. The more we embrace the highs and lows, the easier life flows. It's in the most difficult parts of our journey, where we struggle, that we learn and grow the most.

This rune invites you to embrace it all and see the lesson that comes with each step of the journey.

PAUSE AND REFLECT

Do you consider yourself a glass-half-empty or glass-half-full person? Why?

Call to mind a situation that caused you pain but in retrospect taught you a great deal.

What are some of the greatest obstacles you have overcome thus far in your life?

WRAP UP

We are all here to learn life lessons. When *raido* appears, we are reminded to refrain from judging ourselves too harshly or judging others based on where they are in their unique journey. The more we can ride the wave and know the bad times will pass, the easier our journey becomes.

SOWILO

Letter: S
Pronunciation: SO-will-oh
One-word meaning: Wholeness
Cosmic tie: ☉ ♌

....

Sowilo connects to the **sun**, which rules vitality and individuality. As such, this rune is associated with **Leo**, the most loyal sign of the zodiac.

Modern meaning: We are all here embarking on our own unique journeys with the goal of staying in spiritual alignment. When we are in perfect alignment, we are connected to the universe, our Higher Selves, and our divine maker. In alignment, we feel fulfilled and at peace. This is our natural state as spiritual beings.

Then life comes at us in harsh and unexpected ways. When we feel anger, sadness, rejection, or loneliness, it is a cue that we have slipped into misalignment and have become disconnected from our soul. We try so hard to simply get through the day.

And then . . . we sleep. With sleep comes an energetic reset. We awake in the morning and breathe new breaths. We understand we made it through another day. We walked another mile. We overcame another obstacle. We start the day again in spiritual alignment.

If you are feeling down today, take a moment to meditate or simply nap. Through meditation and rest, we can bring ourselves back into this feeling of wholeness and alignment. The more you practice shifting yourself back to wholeness, the easier it will be for you to remain aligned and feel whole.

PAUSE AND REFLECT

What does being whole mean to you?

In what areas of your life do you feel fulfilled completely?

In what areas of your life do you feel you need to grow?

WRAP UP

When *sowilo* appears, we are reminded that we can spiritually reset every day. Notice that moment of stillness when you first awake, and hold on to it for as long as you can. With practice and focused intention, you can remain in spiritual alignment. In doing so, you will find the peace you seek.

TEIWAZ

↑

Letter: T
Pronunciation: TEE-wawz
One-word meaning: Warrior
Cosmic tie: ♂ ♈

....

Teiwaz is strongly tied to **Mars,** the planet that sparks drive, aggression, and masculine energy. Its corresponding sign is **Aries,** the most spontaneous and restless sign of the zodiac.

Modern meaning: Quieting your mind and stilling your body are skills you must master. Learning to be completely present in conversations, when doing a task, or when relaxing will greatly enhance your emotional well-being. Regret about the past inhibits the joy you can feel in the present. Anxiety about the future creates fear and can prevent us from moving forward.

Release the warrior within. The warrior is completely present. She quietly scans her environment and takes in her surroundings. She doesn't anticipate or fret. She is serene on the inside and the outside. Should trouble arise, she is ready to act. Her power stems from her ability to simply be.

In your mind's eye, see yourself as the warrior: confident, present, strong. Let go of any fleeting thoughts or tendency to multitask. Focus on the moment you are in, and notice how different you feel. This will require practice, but it is a task you can master. Embrace your warrior within.

PAUSE AND REFLECT

What past situations cause you to feel regret?

What future situations cause you anxiety?

Create a "warrior within" affirmation, beginning with "I am . . .," that you repeat throughout the day today to help you release these regrets and fears.

When you feel yourself not being present today, repeat your warrior-within affirmation.

WRAP UP

When *teiwaz* appears, we are encouraged to stop, look, and listen to what is around us. Release regrets from the past and worries for the future. Be in this present moment. Be aware and be still to heighten what you see, sense, and know.

URUZ

ᚢ

Letter: U
Pronunciation: OO-rooze
One-word meaning: Strength
Cosmic tie: ♅≈

....

Uruz is strongly tied to **Uranus**, the planet that evokes sudden change, creativity, individuality, and eccentricity. This rune is connected with **Aquarius**, the most conscious and humanitarian sign of the zodiac.

Modern meaning: Your strength runs deep. You have overcome so many challenges in your life that have made you stronger, steadier, and more capable. Often it is not until we are challenged in some way that we have an opportunity to see for ourselves how strong we actually are.

This rune invites you to take a moment to look back at the road behind you and all the experiences in your life during which you've persevered. Reflect on how far you've come; then share the wisdom of what you've learned with others who feel scared or weak at this time.

The world needs you to continue to build on your strength, speak your truth, and teach others to do the same. We can allow adversity to crush our spirit, or we can use it to make us stronger. You have chosen to become stronger along your journey. You now are beginning to understand that strength is a self-cultivated gift.

Give yourself a hug today for all you have risen above, and pay it forward by sharing your life experiences with someone in need so they can become stronger, too.

You have all the strength you need and will always persevere.

PAUSE AND REFLECT

How do you define strength?

What was the most significant hurdle you have overcome in your life?

What did that experience teach you?

WRAP UP

When *uruz* appears, we are being reminded of our inner power and strength. It is through trying times that our strength is tested and amplified. Call upon *uruz,* and you can weather any storm.

WUNJO

ᚹ

Letter: V, W
Pronunciation: WOO-yo
One-word meaning: Joy
Cosmic tie: ☉ ♌

....

Wunjo connects to the **sun**, which rules vitality and individuality. As such, this rune is associated with **Leo**, the most loyal sign of the zodiac.

Modern meaning: We all possess the ability to experience joy every day. Joy is a natural state of being, in which we feel happy to our core. When we experience joy, we feel deep satisfaction. We are completely present, with no regrets about the past or anxiety about the future. We are comfortable to just be.

However, many of us have mental blocks that prevent us from feeling joy. We may feel mired down by the stress of raising children, financial burdens, conflict at work or school, or disharmony in a personal relationship. We may not think it is possible to choose between feeling stressed or feeling joy, but we do possess that ability.

For example, you can choose to be frustrated while stuck in a traffic jam, or you can choose to turn on the radio and appreciate the unplanned time to sit still and enjoy some music.

Starting with today, see joy as a choice. Joy does not happen to you; you can experience joy any time, as often as you wish. During challenging moments today, close your eyes and ask yourself, "Where is the joy in this moment?" In a stressful moment at work, can your hot cup of coffee be a moment of joy? Can stepping outside to feel the sun on your face give you a moment of pleasure?

Bring your awareness to the pleasure the coffee or sunshine brings you. Embrace that feeling, and invite the joy inside of you. Joy is a choice.

PAUSE AND REFLECT

Name three things that bring you joy.

When you feel joy, where do you feel it in your body?

How can you bring more of these joyful moments into your daily life?

WRAP UP

When *wunjo* appears, we are being encouraged to not take things so seriously. Find the comedy in all situations. Look in the mirror and smile at beautiful you. Be silly! Let your inner child out to laugh, sing, and play.

THURISAZ

ᚦ

Letter: TH
Pronunciation: THOOR-eh-saws
One-word meaning: Gateway
Cosmic tie: ᛖᛗ

....

Thurisaz is strongly connected to **Pluto,** the planet associated with power, transformation, and rebirth. Its astrological counterpart is **Scorpio,** the most intense and sexual of the zodiac signs.

Modern meaning: A new beginning is on the horizon, and with it comes necessary change. Before you can begin this next chapter, you are being called upon to release the things in your life that no longer fit the person you have become.

Be honest with yourself about what you desire from this new chapter. Say goodbye to negative patterns, old hurts, and self-limiting beliefs. Leave them behind as you close the current chapter. This act of release creates space for your emotional and spiritual expansion.

This may also be a time when soul-level contracts with others have been fulfilled. In other words, there may be people in your life who have been on your journey thus far who are not meant to continue to accompany you as you move forward. While this fact may be bittersweet, some goodbyes are necessary and are for the best as you expand and grow.

You are here to live, learn, love, and be the happiest you. It is through releasing what we have outgrown that we make room for beginning anew.

PAUSE AND REFLECT

In what area of your life do you long for a transformational change?

What old hurt might you be holding on to that you need to release?

Who can you talk to throughout this process so you have stability and support as this personal transformation occurs?

WRAP UP

When *thurisaz* appears, we are put on notice to clean out our emotional closets and discard what no longer serves us. It is time to proceed onward to the happier, more enlightened life that is waiting for you just ahead.

EIHWAZ

Letter: Y
Pronunciation: EYE-wawz
One-word meaning: Surrender
Cosmic tie: ♆ ♓

Eihwaz draws from the energy of **Neptune**, the planet associated with idealism, spirituality, surrender, and transcendence. This rune connects strongly to **Pisces**, the wisest and most loving of the zodiac signs.

Modern meaning: Persistence, patience, and perseverance are important at this time. Understand that all things take time, and the most important things in life cannot be rushed. Although you often need to see progress to believe "things are happening," trust that this is a time for allowing things to unfold naturally without applying any form of pressure.

Resist the urge to intervene to make something happen or block something from happening. Sometimes the best action is inaction. Decisions and actions you might take today will look very different later, when you see more and know more. There are too many moving parts at this time to formulate a plan that will play out in your best interest.

Hold on for now; no sudden movements. Pause, wait, and allow more to naturally unfold before you act. You will know when it's time to make a move.

PAUSE AND REFLECT

What is happening in your life right now that makes you want to act, perhaps in haste?

Is there any downside to waiting to act? Why?

Can you discern the difference between reacting in the moment versus responding after you've given something appropriate time to unfold on its own?

WRAP UP

Eihwaz reminds us to stay the course for now. Allow for the big picture to come into focus before you say or do anything. Give it time, and only take action after more details come to light.

ALGIZ

ᛉ

Letter: Y
Pronunciation: ALL-heez
One-word meaning: Protection
Cosmic tie: ♂ᛉ

....

Algiz is strongly tied to **Mars,** the planet that sparks drive, aggression, and masculine energy. Its corresponding sign is **Aries,** the most spontaneous and restless sign of the zodiac.

Modern meaning: Your best interests are being considered and cared for, both in the physical world and in the spiritual world. The time has come to release the worry you are carrying about this area in your life. You are not in it alone, even though it can feel that way sometimes. This is an ideal time for you to take inventory of all your blessings and realize how many times you were scared of a possible negative outcome that never came to be.

Create a personal mantra for today, such as, "Things are always working out for me," or "I have nothing to fear; someone always has my back." Repeat this mantra throughout the day. As you say your mantra aloud, feel your sense of vulnerability dissipate.

You have all the protection you need, and you don't have to worry about your well-being.

PAUSE AND REFLECT

Under what circumstances do you presently feel unsafe, uneasy, or over-come with worry?

To what extent are you driving your own anxiety in this matter?

Who are the people in your life you can call upon during times of distress because you know they have your back?

WRAP UP

Many of the scenarios we fear the most never come to be. *Algiz* reminds us just how much worry we manufacture in our undisciplined minds. You are safe. You are protected. Trust that things always end up working themselves out for the best.

INGWAZ

Letter: NG
Pronunciation: ING-waz
One-word meaning: Fertility
Cosmic tie: ♀♎♉

....

Ingwaz ties to **Venus**, the planet known for its feminine energy, inspiring romance, love, and beauty. As such, this rune is connected with **Libra**, the most balanced of all the signs of the zodiac, and **Taurus**, the most stable of the signs.

Modern meaning: The time has come for something unexpected and amazing to happen. The start of a new chapter of your life is on the horizon. A chance encounter or a simple conversation has the power to spark something significant in your life. Professionally, this could manifest as a new career option or a business partnership opportunity. Personally, this could ignite a new relationship or a particularly meaningful friendship. It could also mean conceiving a new creative idea—or quite literally a pregnancy.

Consider bringing any unresolved affairs or open-ended projects to a resolution so you may act swiftly and decisively when this new opportunity presents itself. Every step you take is on fertile ground. Proceed throughout your day in a state of readiness to receive and respond to the good news coming your way.

PAUSE AND REFLECT

When you think of the words "fertile ground," what is the first thing that comes to mind?

What new project, mindset, or experience do you want to birth?

How will your life change for the better when this new endeavor begins?

WRAP UP

When *ingwaz* appears, we are put on alert that something new is days or hours away from us. We have done all the necessary work, and now comes the reward. Be open to and fully ready for what is about to come.

UNKNOWN

The blank rune represents the Unknown. It means that either the foresight you desire cannot be shared, as the outcome is not yet clear, or it is in your best interest for the clarity you seek not to be shared at this time. Be patient; more will be revealed to you when the time is right.

If you pull the Unknown as your daily pull, simply draw another rune.

PART IV

MOVING
FORWARD

Now that you've been working with the runes on a daily basis, you can see how powerful your left and right brain can be when you effortlessly tap in to both your creative, intuitive side and your fact-based, rational side. You have gained invaluable insight by reviewing your life's significant moments, challenging situations, and key relationships. Now that you have established a clear daily practice and have learned to step away from any situation, pause, and evaluate, no longer will you take things so personally or be a victim of circumstance.

You now have a new method for grounding yourself, too. You know more about life, and more importantly, you know more about yourself. When we come from a place of knowing ourselves, that is when we are the most self-assured and confident with standing in our truth. When we know that we've got our own back, we understand that we can overcome any obstacle in our way. We become unafraid to admit to ourselves how we feel and what we want, and to back it up with the courage to say it out loud without fearing rejection and loss.

We all enjoy having love and support from others in our lives, but the most powerful gift we can give ourselves is unconditional self-love and a sense of self-worth. Someone else can repeatedly tell us we're lovable and amazing, but we need to see it, feel it, and know it for ourselves for it to be real.

The runes enable this connection between our Human Self and our Higher Self. In using the runes to have these daily conversations with ourselves, the fog slowly lifts, and we step into awareness. We step into clarity. We step into us.

Chances are, you focused on a particular area of your life over these last several weeks, such as a relationship or a career matter. Do you have complete clarity now? If not, you may wish to continue with your daily practice or even use the runes repeatedly throughout your day to ask questions and receive immediate answers. If you feel you now know what you need to know about that one area, consider your next area of focus. By keeping a simple journal, you can launch a "Next Thirty Days" effort and track the guidance you obtain from the runes.

You can also call on the energy of Freya for matters of the heart and relationships, Heimdall for clarity and balanced insight, and Tyr for courage and confidence. Remember that their stories have been passed down over the centuries to remind us that we all possess the strengths of Freya, Heimdall, and Tyr within ourselves. Our heroes and heroine needed to face and overcome adversity to achieve what they wanted, and we are no different.

Another way to further adopt the runes into your life is to teach a friend how to use them. Or, when you are consulted for advice, you can pull a rune stone to inspire the highest level of advice you can offer a friend. As I mentioned earlier, it is possible to simply close your eyes and see a rune symbol in your mind's eye rather than using a bag of physical rune stones. Everyone's process is different.

INSTANT RUNIC FRIENDS AROUND THE WORLD

If you are craving more information about the runes and want to explore with other enthusiasts, I recommend using social media, as the runes have a devoted following online.

Beginning with Facebook, here are three closed groups that both inspire and educate me:

- **Runes for Runesters**, moderated by Wylde Hunter, is a great one if you would like to learn more about the history and traditions of the Old Norse people. Its approximately seven thousand members are interesting people who share their knowledge and passions related to the runes. You will encounter some people whom I consider to be purists, who may not believe that innovation and runes belong together; but hey, to each their own. We are all here to learn and have fun, and there is a lot of expertise in this group.

- I also really enjoy **All Pagan, Norse & Heathens.** There is a more intimate and familial feel in this smaller group of about two thousand members. People will post pictures of their new-born "baby Vikings" or ask for prayers when someone is hurt or ill. Group moderator Lee Mellings does a nice job of creating community.

*   **Norse Rune Writing/Translating** is another cool group, with around fifteen thousand members. Its moderator, Quinn Forman, is very diligent about overseeing the group to be sure that cultural and attitudinal differences are respected, which is not always the case in closed groups. Members often post when they want help translating things they find.

On YouTube, you can watch scholar Dr. Jackson Crawford. A professor at the University of Colorado and expert in all things Old Norse, Crawford has more than eighty-five thousand loyal followers on his two-year-old channel. He is a great presenter and published author. If academia is your thing, Jackson is your guy.

There is also a fascinating TEDx Talk about the runes by Mark Kinders, the vice president of public affairs at the University of Oklahoma. In his talk, Kinders explores rune carvings found in North America. He is also the vice president of the American Association for Runic Studies, a nonprofit organization committed to promoting scholarly research on the runes in Europe and North America.

FORMING YOUR OWN CIRCLE

Alternatively, to keep your positive momentum going, consider forming a rune circle with positive, supportive people who share your desire to live authentically. Just as important as turning inward for divine guidance, we need to model the way for like-minded people by lifting each other up and encouraging each other to stay on our paths to personal fulfillment and happiness. I find that the happiest people I know get shot down by others who envy their freedom and bright light—something Freya could relate to.

In creating a rune circle that meets once or twice a month, you are creating a safe space to be both great and vulnerable without fear of judgment. As a result of beta-testing this book, I created my own rune circle with six incredible people who are my confidants and soul sisters. These amazing people are entrepreneurial and fearless in their pursuit of living their lives how they want to in the business world, despite the prevalence of conformist nay-sayers.

My rune circle tribe consists of a holistic business coach, a women's empowerment and conflict resolution coach, an intuitive writer/painter, a communications consultant, a co-owner of a six-hundred-person human services company that she patiently co-leads with her spouse, a budding entrepreneur who is on what I call her "final year farewell tour of corporate," and a car-wash owner. We meet every other Friday via group video chat and share stories of what patterns are appearing in our rune pulls and what amazing outcomes we are manifesting. We enjoy being there for each other in a way that allows us to heal from old hurts and grow as divine beings.

Another way to keep the momentum going is to download the Runa Reading app, which provides an easy way to do your daily rune pull and seek runic guidance through the convenience of a digital pull. You can journal directly in the app to track your journey. You can also meet like-minded goddesses if you want to expand your contacts and perhaps make new friends for your own rune circle.

Whatever you do, I encourage you to keep learning, growing, mentoring, and sharing. I hope your thirty-day journey has brought you clarity, confidence, and happiness. And may your next thirty days be even better!

Illustration by George Peters Designs

EPILOGUE

When I first began writing *Rune Reading Your Life,* my ten-year-old Samoyed, Kodi—whom I lovingly referred to as my "first-born"—was a fixture in my daily writing routine. Kodi would wake up with me at four a.m., accompany me to the kitchen as I brewed my ritual pot of coffee, then follow me into my home office and settle in by my feet as I tapped away on my laptop until daybreak. One of the oldest known breeds descended from the white wolf, Samoyeds are highly intelligent, mischievous, and vocal. Kodi was all of that, which made me love him even more. I would tell people that Kodi's tagline is *I do what I want.* My dad would say, "Kodi is just like his mom." Perhaps!

When Kodi fell ill in January of 2019, his tests were deemed inconclusive, but the specialist thought he had stomach cancer, intestinal cancer, or both. I couldn't believe it. In my daily prayer and meditations, I was reassured that he would be fine. Despite this, we began to treat Kodi with an aggressive chemotherapy protocol. He responded well for nearly four months, and then within thirty-six hours, his health rapidly declined.

This can't be possible, I thought. *I've been connecting with Kodi's soul in my meditations, and he told me he was just fine.*

On the last morning of his life, we sat on the couch near the fireplace with his head in my lap. I felt his love for me so strongly. It was if time stood still. I went into meditation and asked to connect to Kodi's soul again. He lovingly told me that he was my soul mate and that he could come back in any form I wanted him to. I told him how much I'd loved our eleven years together—our hikes, road trips, early mornings—and that I wanted him to come back as another Samoyed. Without hesitation, he told me he would "be right back." He went on to tell me he was not afraid, and being near me made him happy. I hugged him and thanked him for the joy he brought to my life.

The same week that Kodi transitioned, baby Kanu was conceived in a town seventy-five miles away. The rune *kanu*, as you now know, represents being open to new possibilities and encourages us to allow life to unfold naturally. Kanu is now sixteen weeks old and sleeping near my desk as I type these words. Kanu is Kodi in a young, strong, new body. The soul is all-knowing and infinite. One look in Kanu's eyes, and I can see it is Kodi.

PHOTO CREDIT: BRANDON WABBLE

Kodi   Kanu

More than ever before, I believe that absolutely anything is possible when you hold love in your heart and have faith that everything you could ever wish for can be, if you simply believe.

Be open. Trust. Believe.

With love and gratitude,
Delanea

RECOMMENDED READING

Blum, Ralph. *The Book of Runes: A Handbook for the Use of an Ancient Oracle.* New York: St. Martin's Press, 1983.

Davidson, H. R. Ellis. *Pagan Scandinavia.* New York: Thames and Hudson, 1967.

DuBois, Thomas. *Nordic Religions in the Viking Age.* Philadelphia: University of Pennsylvania, 1960.

Dumèzil, Georges. *Gods of the Ancient Northmen.* Berkeley: University of California, 1973.

Farnell, Kim. *Runes: Plain and Simple.* Charlottesville, VA: Hampton Roads Publishing, 2006.

Findell, Martin. *Runes: Ancient Scripts.* Los Angeles: Getty Publications, 2015.

Flowers, Stephen. *Runes and Magic: Magical Formulaic Elements in the Older Runic Tradition.* New York: Peter Lang, 1986.

Fries-Mandrake, Jan. *Helrunar: A Manual of the Runic Magick.* Newburyport, MA: Red Wheel/Weiser, 1997.

Lindow, John. *Norse Mythology: A Guide to the Gods, Heroes, Rituals, and Beliefs.* Oxford, UK: Oxford University Press, 2001.

McKinnell, John. *Meeting the Other in Norse Myth and Legend.* Suffolk, UK: Boydell and Brewer, 2005.

Melville, Francis. *The Book of Runes: Interpreting the Ancient Stones.* New York: Wellfleet Press, 2016.

Mountfort, Paul Rhys. *Nordic Runes: Understanding, Casting, and Interpreting the Ancient Viking Oracle.* Rochester, NY: Destiny Books, 2003.

Page, R. I. *Runes: Reading the Past.* Berkeley: University of California Press, 1987.

Pollington, Stephen. *Rudiments of Runelore.* Little Downham, UK: Anglo Saxon Books, 2008.

Rydberg, Viktor. *Teutonic Mythology: Gods and Goddesses of the Northland.* Urbana-Champaign: University of Chicago Press, 1906.

Thorsson, Edred. *Futhark: A Handbook of Rune Magic.* San Francisco: Red Wheel/Weiser, 1984.

———. *Runecaster's Handbook: The Well of Wyrd.* San Francisco: Red Wheel/Weiser, 1999.

———. *Runelore: The Magic, History, and Hidden Codes of the Runes.* San Francisco: Red Wheel/Weiser, 1987.

INDEX

ABOUT THE AUTHOR

Delanea Davis is the active managing partner and co-founder of two thriving businesses: Experience Design International, an international management consulting business, and Cloud9 Online, a health and healing technology business. As a CEO and advocate for developing leadership skills in women, she has coached and mentored people through workshops and in individual sessions throughout her career. Davis holds a bachelor's degree in political science and communications, has an advanced degree in research methodology, and is a certified generalist in organizational psychology. She believes that when one finds the courage to look within and embrace one's inner Truth with confidence, anything is possible.

About North Atlantic Books

North Atlantic Books (NAB) is a 501(c)(3) nonprofit publisher committed to a bold exploration of the relationships between mind, body, spirit, culture, and nature. Founded in 1974, NAB aims to nurture a holistic view of the arts, sciences, humanities, and healing. To make a donation or to learn more about our books, authors, events, and newsletter, please visit www.northatlanticbooks.com.